Michael's candid, detailed, and often hilarious breakdown of the audition process is a must-read for actors at all levels. Whatever your background in training, you'll find something in here that will change your perspective and give you a healthier and more sane approach to auditions. —Ryan C., Amazon

I've read a lot of books on auditioning and this is by far the best one! Brutally honest and super helpful. —Anonymous, Amazon

A must-read . . . helps you take a more reasoned and logical approach to auditioning. —Charlene C. Sloan, Amazon

Great advice and encouraging insight to auditions, done with logic and wit. —Thezoo232, Goodreads

An invaluable resource that should be a part of every actor's toolkit. —Keith Kelly

This one is a game-changer! —Riley, Goodreads

A must-read for professional actors. If this is the only book on the business of acting that you ever read, you'll be more successful—and, more importantly, less of an anxious actor-y mess—because of it. I can't recommend this to you enough. —Joshua Grisetti, Goodreads

Essential reading. —Samantha S., Amazon

Killer advice from a pro! I wish I had read this a couple of years ago. —D. W. Griffith, Amazon

I have attended Michael's workshop a few times, and this is a perfect representation of what he teaches. Now you can read it wherever you happen to be. Grab yourself an index card and a pen, and read this book before your next appointment! —Siskita, Amazon

Audition Psych 101

cover design: Tim Gabor (www.timgabor.com)
copy editor: Mindi White (ammaze@aol.com)
photos: Leslie Hassler (www.lesliehassler.com)

Published by Gatekeeper Press
2167 Stringtown Rd, Suite 109
Columbus, OH 43123-2989
www.GatekeeperPress.com

Columbus, Ohio

ISBN (paperback): 9781642376128
eISBN: 9781642376111

Printed in the United States of America

A Refreshing Approach to the Dreaded Process

Michael Kostroff

gatekeeper press

Columbus, Ohio

For Billie Shepard, world-class actor, teacher, and friend, and the mother of Audition Psych 101. "Teach an audition class," she said. "But I have nothing to teach," I protested. "Dummy!" she said, "Every time I have an audition, I call you and you give me some golden piece of advice that saves my ass. Write it down!"

THANKS

I owe a special debt of gratitude to my favorite editors, Jenny Kostroff, Patrick Richwood, and Sue Judin, and my crackerjack copy editor Mindi White. I also want to thank my extraordinary cover artist Tim Gabor for his patience with my endless tinkering, and for delivering the most perfect book cover I could ever ask for.

I'm grateful as well to the many actors, casting directors, and others who contributed their thoughts on the subject of auditioning.

Finally, my heartfelt thanks to the thousands who've attended the Audition Psych 101 workshops over the years. Your participation has helped me to hone the concepts in this book, and to communicate them more clearly and effectively.

FOREWORD

If your auditions feel more like trials than performances, you are not alone. Michael Kostroff has been where you are. For years he walked through the fires of auditioning, barely surviving. Believing auditions didn't have to be torture, Michael gradually discovered some pertinent truths, then tested his theories, using himself as a guinea pig. And something remarkable happened. He began to really enjoy auditioning! And yes, he also began to be successful at it. He seemed to have turned the audition process on its head. And that's lucky for us.

I have been teaching actors of all levels for over thirty years. I founded five acting workshops in four states, taught acting at San Jose State University (where I earned my Masters in Theatre), as well as at San Jose Repertory Theatre and Voice One in San Francisco. The point is, I've been teaching long enough to recognize exceptional teaching talent when I see it. And that brings us back to Michael Kostroff. The gods were good to Kostroff. He's not only a brilliant actor and writer but, what's most unusual, he can really teach.

Kostroff and I met in 1997 at San Jose Rep when we were cast together in Neil Simon's *Laughter on the 23rd Floor*. Working with him was a joy and an education. He was open, supportive, and generous. We became friends. And so, over the years when I needed help with an audition, I'd call Michael. Like most of my fellow actors and students, I could be plagued by the unwelcome voices of self-doubt, nerves, fear, second-guessing, self-evaluation, and people pleasing. These rude voices could really diminish the audition experience.

Working with Michael was magical. I immediately realized he had—in a gentle, fun manner—realigned my attitude toward the entire process. Quite suddenly I noticed I was looking forward to my auditions as a chance to act, play, and show my best self. It was a huge adjustment. Numerous times I said, "You should teach!" And numerous times he said, "Awwww, no." That went on far too long, because he's authentically modest. Fortunately for you, I am authentically relentless. Ultimately, I prevailed. We brought Michael to San Jose Rep to teach a one-night class, and *Audition Psych 101* was born. He teaches all over the country now. To this day, my students and fellow actors come up to me and tell me how their attitudes toward auditioning have improved and how much more they book and enjoy their auditions since attending the class. They consistently mention how simple, accessible, and—most importantly—fun Michael's techniques are to use. Kostroff has elegantly hit on a simple truth: most of what we hate about auditioning is in our heads!

If you're not able to attend his Audition Psych 101 workshop in person, read this book. If you are able to attend his Audition Psych 101 workshop in person, read this book anyway. Then enjoy your next audition!

—Billie Shepard

TABLE OF CONTENTS

PREFACE

This is not an acting book. It's also not a book about how to break into show business, get noticed, or get an agent. In fact, it's not even your typical book on the subject of auditions, though that's the sole topic; there's very little here about improving your cold reading skills, choosing audition materials, scene analysis, camera technique, or any of the other usual audition-related subjects. This book is about one specific element of the audition process: the mental part—the weird shit that goes on in actors' heads as we face what is easily one of the oddest ways anyone has ever applied for a job.

It's my belief (and my experience as a working professional) that much of what goes wrong for us in auditions has less to do with talent, acting ability, or learned skills than with things like nerves, insecurities, second guessing, fear of judgment, overanalyzing . . . that kind of stuff. (Any of that sound familiar?) I think the place we run into the biggest problems is in the space that sits between our ears, and that the way we *think* and *feel* about auditioning can be our worst obstacle. This is even more so once actors reach a professional level. Beginners and amateurs might botch the basics and exhibit more nervousness, but for people who more or less know what they're doing, and for whom the stakes are a bit higher, the mental gremlins can pose an even greater threat, taking us down hard and blocking access to our best work.

I also believe there's a considerable amount of mythology that actors build around the idea of auditioning. And everyone just sort of blindly follows along, never questioning certain widely held falsehoods. On these pages, I'm going to offer some reality-based alternatives to those bizarre myths.

By the way, there's a reason that I'm uniquely qualified to teach this stuff. It isn't because of my modest bit of professional success or because I'm some sort of shaman. My unique qualification is simply this: I was once *impossibly* bad at auditioning. I'm not being humble or coy or cute when I say that. I give you my word—I stunk. I was *monumentally* awkward. I felt like I'd snuck in and didn't belong there. (Anyone else ever feel like that? Or is it just me?) Everything about my demeanor was one big apology. I was so anxious that I couldn't focus at all. And afterwards, sometimes I couldn't even remember what I did or said in the room; it was like a blackout. I'm sure I came across as overwhelmed, terror-stricken and miserable, and—would you believe it?—I never got cast. Never. Strange, huh? I guess no one wanted to hire the sweaty weirdo with the blank gaze and the quivering voice. Go figure.

Luckily, I was blessed with an analytical nature, and so I was somehow able, over many years, to pick apart and sort through the various elements and micro-moments of the audition process, figure out where things were going wonky, and eventually get to the place where I could present myself comfortably and finally, really enjoy auditioning. Now I teach my colleagues how to do the same thing. (Never would have seen that one coming in a million years.)

This book is based on my Audition Psych 101 workshop, which I've presented all across the country, to actors at all levels, as a means by which to convey my discoveries and give actors new approaches to the psychological challenges of auditioning. What's been particularly illuminating for me is seeing how universal these challenges are for us. We do a lot of laughing in my workshops, mostly because people recognize the craziness and angst I talk about, and they're surprised to find that the little demons in their heads visit their fellow actors as well. It's a relief to know that so many of us go through the same crap. A number of years ago, I was presenting Audition Psych 101 to a group of actors in Hollywood, and a young woman in the back kept giggling. I finally asked her why. "It's just so freeing!" she laughed.

I hope you'll find this book both freeing and giggle-worthy, and that it will lead you to a place where you can honestly say, as I can, that auditioning is one of the great joys of being an actor.

(Uh-uh-uh! I heard that skepticism in your head. Give me a chance, willya? This is just the Preface!)

THE CASE FOR NEGATIVE THINKING

I want to make this absolutely clear up front. I don't believe in positive thinking . . . at least not of the new-agey, say-nice-things-and-they'll-happen variety. Not to get too far off course here, I'll just say I believe that particular type of positive thinking is a dangerous and irresponsible philosophy. (On that subject, I recommend Barbara Ehrenreich's book, *Bright-sided—How Positive Thinking is Undermining America*, which demonstrates just how dangerous and irresponsible it can be.)

Now, don't misunderstand; I'm very much in favor of having a positive *attitude*. That's something very different. I believe it's good for our mental health when we count our blessings, avoid complaining, believe in the possibility of favorable outcomes, assess our strengths, stop and smell the roses, appreciate what we have, and make the absolute best of our circumstances.

But this business of believing we can *will* things into existence, create things with words—this idea that picturing something makes it happen—is one that worries me, and one that, I believe, doesn't serve you well in an audition scenario. Because here's what's true: if twelve guys in an audition waiting room, all up for the same role, are each affirming that the role is his, positively visualizing showing up on set and filming it, guess what? *Even still*, only one of them will get the job. And what of the eleven other poor souls? On top of not getting the gig, they're now left feeling like they failed to visualize properly.

I also reject the popular philosophy that says everything happens for the best. Ask any victim of violence, anyone whose loved one died way too young, or anyone who's ever been defrauded. Ask someone who's starving, or who never found love. See if these people believe everything happens for the best. Some things in this life truly suck. Period. And if there's one profession that proves it, it's show business.

I know there may be some who are offended by this point of view. That's not my aim. And if you're a believer in creative visualization, affirmations, and such, you needn't feel like this book isn't for you. You'll find plenty of value here. But as for me, I worry about actors going out into the very real world of auditioning with a reliance on such fanciful beliefs.

I am, as you'll learn, far more comfortable with brutally blunt reality, warts and all. And that's a big part of Audition Psych 101. The reality is, we don't have control. We never did. So if, at times, it sounds like I'm espousing positive thinking (of the just-believe-and-it-will-happen variety), trust me, I'm not. I'm never going to encourage you to convince yourself of something that isn't reliably real. Instead, we're going to take a hard look at those realities and see if we can find better ways to manage them by applying good old-fashioned logic, honesty, and practicality.

I believe in something I've come to call the Negative Positive. It goes like this. Get brutally honest about the situation; don't sugarcoat it. Call it what it is. Then figure out how best to work with those realities. Like if you know you're coming down with the flu, rather than suppressing or denying that awareness (and rather than trying to "positive think" it away), just admit it, go with it, treat it, and get through it. Meanwhile, accept the fact that—like it or not—you may need to miss work, and relish the opportunity to catch up on your TV viewing.

And you want to hear something bizarre? Sometimes the harshest realities, if you'll dare to face them, offer hidden perks. The truth shall set you free. (But I'm getting ahead of myself.)

WHAT WAS THAT THING?

Now, before we go any further, I want you to go get an index card. If you don't have one handy, stop reading, get one, and come back. I hand them out at my workshops as people enter, and yours is about to become your new best friend. Here's why. At some point while reading this book, you'll come across something brilliant—some story or tip or quote or technique that will make a light bulb switch on in your head. "My God!" you'll think, "This is *exactly* what I needed to conquer my audition challenges! Thank you, Michael Kostroff! I'll never forget your wise advice!"

Yes, you will. You'll forget exactly the thing you promised yourself you'd never forget. And you know *when* you'll forget it? I'll answer this one for you. You'll forget it while waiting outside a casting office, about to audition. "Damn it!" you'll think, "What was that thing I was supposed to remember that was going to help me keep my head together in this situation?!?"

That's what the index card is for. I want you to write on it *only* those things that specifically resonate for you, the things that make you say, "Aha!" It might be a lot or it might be a little. I've seen people write down one word, and I've seen people take several cards and staple them together into a little booklet. Doesn't matter. What matters is that you write down the stuff that addresses *your* challenges in ways that make sense for you.

And then bring that card with you to every audition. Review it while waiting, or on the way there (unless you're driving; that's not so good). I swear to you, it helps. It puts the words you wanted to remember right there in front of you. And it saves you the stress of trying to remember something at a time when you may have other things on your mind. I often hear from actors who tell me that these stupid little pieces of paper saved their asses at auditions.

Now, I know you're tempted to read on and ignore this instruction. But please trust my experience on this one. Do yourself a favor. Go get an index card. I'll wait.

❧

CHAPTER ONE

An Old Cliché about the World's Second-Oldest Profession[1]

I'm going to go way out on a limb here and say I'm probably not the first person to suggest that professional acting is a crazy business. I'm sure back in ancient Greece there were guys talking about it.

> "Murray, the play is based on my life! What do you *mean* they won't even see me for the role? It was *written* for me!"

> "What can I tell you, Irving? It's a crazy business."

It's such an old cliché, in fact, that we no longer give it much thought. It's something everyone knows. Even people who

---

[1] Prostitution has long been called "the world's oldest profession." The dubious honor of "world's second-oldest profession" has been assigned to politics, espionage, journalism, and, quite often, acting.

don't know the first thing about our profession will tell you, with great authority, "Oh you're an actor? Crazy business." ("Uh, thanks. Can I just have my sandwich?")

But I wonder: when was the last time you examined that idea? *Why* do we say that acting is a crazy business? Let's do that now, as this sets the stage for much of what's to come. Let's take a look at just how crazy the acting profession looks when you compare it with "normal" professions like banking, truck driving, real estate, manufacturing, sales, graphic design, auto repair, business consulting, and other such sensible endeavors.

At this point, I should warn you—all the most depressing parts of this book are at the beginning. So get ready. It's about to get bleak and discouraging. We'll re-emerge into the light, I promise. But we have to get very honest first, and build on what's really true, rather than some more encouraging fantasy.

OK . . . so, why is the acting business a crazy business? First of all, the job itself is crazy. What exactly is it that we actors do? In short, we pretend to be other people. And that's considered a job. Spies, con artists, and us—that's our job, passing as someone else. Actually, I have to amend that; we're not always pretending to be people. Sometimes, we pretend to be animals. Sometimes, if things get artsy and experimental enough, we might portray fire, the year 1911, euphoria, or God knows what else. In fact, we may actually play a character called "God Knows What Else." Colleagues, I'm not kidding around here. I have, in the course of my dignified career as a working actor, played a talking beaver, a dollar bill, and yes, a can of asparagus. For money. This is the profession we're in. This is what we do.

Most employed individuals—the vast majority—go to offices, or stores, or restaurants, or factories, or laboratories, and do actual, tangible work. They make things, supervise things, fix, clean, deliver, or sell things. Often, there's paperwork involved. Phone calls. Meetings. Emails. Us? We deal in things that float invisibly in the air somewhere—fluff, wisps of falsehood, imaginary situations. We claim to create "moments" from groups of words that are spoken out loud and then lost forever in the ether. That's what we provide—acting, something you can neither see nor touch nor eat nor use to prop a door open. Our job description? Replicating behavior . . . while people watch. And sometimes, someone pays us for that. As jobs go, you cannot tell me that isn't just plain weird.

And what makes it an even crazier job is the level of intensity we sometimes reach in our attempts to create this intangible, indefinable stuff. Relationships have been ruined arguing over which acting choices were most "truthful" and which ones were "false." I once had an angry, passionate, half-hour argument with a director over whether I should pick up the phone *before* the line, "Thank God I'm here, this telephone is dead," or in the middle. What the hell do we do for a living?

Secondly, it's a crazy profession from a practical standpoint, and we all know it. Becoming an actor will never be a sensible business plan because, as I always say, the math sucks. To put it in economic terms: the supply outweighs the demand, and it does so by such a huge ratio it's almost comical. Almost. (It's somewhat less humorous to those of us trying to make a living.) There are always too many actors for too few jobs. No one has ever uttered the words, "Gosh. I wish there were more actors. There just don't seem to be enough." The SAG-AFTRA statistics indicate that somewhere around ninety percent of its membership is unemployed at any given time. Ninety percent! How do you like them odds? And now, thanks to advancements in online technology, much of casting has moved to the Internet, giving access to even more hopefuls. An agent friend of mine told me that a recent casting breakdown for one role in a commercial attracted—are you sitting down?—*seven thousand* responses. With competition like that for a single role, it's insane to think we could possibly make a living at this stuff. It's just bad math. And this glut of available actors affects more than just our chances of getting employment; it affects nearly every aspect of our profession. Getting an agent? Incredibly difficult. Gaining respect? Good luck. Even getting a *shot* at getting work (i.e., an audition) can be nearly impossible.

And the ugly truth is that most of the time, even when you *do* manage to get an audition, you don't get the job. Again, that's just the math of it. The odds of booking an acting job are insanely slim. I'm an actor who works a fair amount, and you know what? Most of the time, I don't get the job. Let's just be honest about this, can we? I mean, it's just us actors here; we don't have to impress anyone. Here's an unvarnished fact: we mostly don't get hired.

Like I said, it's a crazy business.

My friend Mark is a salesman. "Kostroff," he tells me, "You and I are in the same business." "Oh, yeah? How so?" says I, and Mark says, "You and I are both in the failure business." Naturally, I was appalled. "Hear me out," he continued, "When I go on a sales call, I *know* that the chances of making a sale are slim to none. Most people will say no to my pitch. That's a built-in fact. A given. Failing is the accepted norm. My highest goal is to fail less than the *other* people in the failure business. That's the gig." And damn it, he's right. Getting any work at all as an actor is a minor miracle. *Not* getting work is the *accepted norm.* Fun, huh? So, the acting profession is a crazy one in terms of practicality.

But what's also crazy—maybe the craziest part—is the relative lack of any sort of pattern in who gets hired. In our business, compared to other businesses, there is far less correlation between merit and success. I'm sorry, but there just is. Does the best actor always get the job? No. The most professional? No. A tax consultant has to be good at her work and be personable toward clients or she probably won't have much of a career. But, not infrequently, the untalented actor who never took a class stars while the classically trained genius plays the fourth soldier from the left. The selfish, belligerent, pain-in-the-ass diva gets offered film after film, at an escalating salary, while the cooperative team player waits for her big break.

In our field, unlike most others, we also don't have a reliable, linear progression for how one builds toward success. An aspiring plumber, I imagine, would start by going to plumbing school, then he'd buy tools, maybe apprentice with an experienced pro for a while, then branch out on his own, advertise, build word of mouth, and so forth. And if he's good at plumbing, and his prices are reasonable, his customers will most likely invite him back to plumb again when the need arises, and thus he'll build his clientele. It's just that simple. And most "normal" professions share a similar logic. There are steps to follow. We don't have those.

For us, there's also no such thing as "moving up in the company." If you got hired to work in a bank, you might start off as a teller, and if you were good at that, you might get promoted to customer service rep, then maybe loan officer, branch manager, regional manager, and so on. There's a sequence and, at least *sometimes*, promotion correlates to talent and experience. The teller doesn't become the regional manager without working his way up the ladder and proving his worth.

We have no such progression. There are no proven steps. You could start in the middle and move to the bottom. You could start at the bottom and stay at the bottom. You could bounce back and forth between wild success and miserable failure, and that would all be fairly standard for our business. And, while a well-developed resumé certainly helps, it's not as if that offers any reliably predictable results. Right?

Even success itself doesn't offer reliably predictable results. If you own a car company and your car is voted Car of the Year several years running by Motor Trend, you can buy that eighth house you always wanted, knowing you can count on sales to go up. Conversely, the seasoned actor who wins an Academy Award—the highest honor we've got—may find himself unemployed for years after being acknowledged as *one of the best in his field*. It's horrible but true. In our business, successful demonstration of superior ability *does not* equal job security. You doubt that? Anyone remember Sammy Williams? Won the Tony Award for *A Chorus Line*. And barely worked after that. He ended up becoming a florist. I know another Tony winner, a supremely talented star who, only a few years after winning, had to start making hats as a sideline because she couldn't manage to land a gig. How about Brenda Fricker? Best Supporting Actress in 1989 for *My Left Foot*? Anyone?

The fact is, there's very little in our profession that is logical, linear, predictable, or consistent. There's very little you can count on with any assurance, very little that can be tracked, charted, or controlled. Compared to other professions, there seems to be much less of a pattern, much less of a progression, and fewer reliable rules. And decisions about who gets hired are subjective, inconsistent, and bound by neither fairness nor merit nor seniority—things that regularly factor into hiring in other professions. I told you we were going to get honest.

OK, show of hands. How many of you have gone on auditions where you *nailed* it, and you didn't get the job? OK, now, how many of you have gone on auditions where you *sucked* . . . and *gotten* the job? Lots of you, I'm guessing. I rest my case.

It's crazy. I once auditioned for *Charmed*, for the role of a bank manager. I was the first one in. After my audition, as I was gathering my things, I heard the casting assistant addressing the *other* guys auditioning for the bank manager, in an exasperated tone. "Guys, please don't play it like . . . "

and went on to describe what I'd just done. Well, kiss that one goodbye, right? Nope. Booked it. Explain *THAT*!

By the way, because I understand how random this all is, I do not make the mistake of assuming that I'm some great actor just because I work a lot in television. Whenever I'm on TV, I picture some other, far more talented, better-trained actor sitting at home in his living room watching me and yelling, "Who's *this* guy? Ugh! He sucks!"

As former screenwriter, now licensed psychotherapist and author Dennis Palumbo has said so brilliantly, "The law of cause and effect works everywhere in the universe . . . except in Hollywood."

The weird truth is, on those all-too-rare occasions when we do get hired, we're not really sure why.

And yet we actors are very superstitious. Holy chicken bones, are we superstitious. When you book a job, what are the first things your fellow actors want to know after they begrudgingly congratulate you? "Who's your agent?" "How'd you get that?" "What did you wear?" "What did you say in the room?" They're thinking that if they had your agent and your outfit and did exactly what you did, they'd be booking jobs like this one. That's pure superstition. Years ago, while waiting to audition for a commercial, I overheard another actor tell his friend, "You know, I've never once booked a commercial when I've worn a white shirt to the audition." This guy had developed a belief that white shirts were cursed. And you know what? I've never worn a white shirt to a commercial audition since. We're superstitious!

In spite of the claims of many a "Break into the Business" seminar, there are no Ten Proven Steps to Guaranteed Success. There are no sure-fire job-getting techniques, nor highly guarded secret methods known only to those of us who work. There is nothing remotely like a reliable plan for getting an acting job. The whole thing is just this weird long shot.

But then, sometimes, on very rare occasions, something magical takes place. Who knows why? Maybe the planets and stars align, maybe you wear the right shirt, and you somehow manage to do this crazy audition thing and not fall apart, and someone actually gets what you're doing, the heavens part, the angels sing, lightning strikes twice in the same place, and a nearly impossible thing happens. You actually book a job . . . and you are employed . . . as a professional actor . . .

For a day.

A day. That's a good job for an actor. Sometimes you get lucky and ooh, it's a whole week. If you're in theatre—wonder of wonders—it might be several weeks. And if you hit the jackpot and get a TV series or a Broadway show or tour, you might possibly find yourself employed for several years. But that's a pretty unusual acting gig, wouldn't you say? Mostly, they're over before you know it and you're back to looking for employment—employment that's next to impossible to obtain.

Are you nuts? Do you know how long you can keep that job at Wal-Mart? Or as a bank teller? Or as a doctor or an accountant? Maybe for the rest of your working life. Talk about security! We don't have anything like that kind of security in this crazy business. We book that one-day job and start high-fiving, hugging, buying a round of drinks, and posting the good news on social media. One day of employment. That's a major score. Why would anyone want this stupid life?

(Here's a fun fact for you. According to a 2014 report by the Bureau of Labor Statistics, today's average American worker stays at a job for 4.6 years, then leaves *by choice* for *another* job. They say it's a trend: "job hopping," they call it. Oh, the irony. The same job for 4.6 years? We'd kill for that kind of longevity.)

Now, not only is it a crazy business, with crazy odds, little hiring logic, and insanely brief periods of employment, but it's also a business that, for some reason, seems to attract a disproportionate number of crazy *people*. I don't have any scientific proof on this, or any research statistics; it's only an opinion based on observation. But come on. It's just us here. No one's listening in. Let's be honest about this, once and for all. Overall, we're a rather odd group. We're moody. We're insecure. We're weirdly child-like. We're sensitive. We're prone to think people don't like us. We're spacy and flaky. We get overwhelmed. We get obsessive. I'm not saying we're *all* crazy. But proportionately, do you think there are as many roofers, golfers, insurance adjusters, or Styrofoam peanut manufacturers who are on antidepressants, in therapy, recovering addicts, survivors of terrible childhoods, neurotics, bipolar, paranoid, or just plain loony as there are actors who are thus afflicted? We're nuts! I mean, is it just me? Am I the only basket case? Or have you noticed, as I have, that our business seems to be a mecca for mental cases? Scratch the surface, and you'll find that a huge number of us are deeply troubled . . . but in kind of a charming way. Sometimes not so charming.

At one of my workshops, I was puzzled by the presence of a woman who'd been scowling from the moment I started talking. She sat near the front, with her arms crossed, glowering at me from under her knitted eyebrows, as if daring me to cross her. She looked so suspicious and so vigilantly judgmental that I wondered why she'd even come. When I mentioned that I thought actors were crazy, she erupted. "They are NOT crazy!" she said in a funny accent. "Actors are WONDERFUL!" "Oh, no...I agree," I said gently. "I *love* actors. I just think we're a little crazy." "They are NOT crazy!" she repeated, escalating her threatening tone. "They can HEAL people with their MINDS." "OK, lady," I thought. "Thanks for clearing that up." Shortly thereafter, she stormed out and never returned. I rest my case.

Among the various brands of crazy in our midst is one that a lot of performers share: massive insecurity. The outside world tends to think that actors are egotistical. But you and I know that's not typically true, is it? On the contrary, it seems most of us believe we're mediocre most of the time. Even when we like our own work, it's still not quite good enough. I liked myself on *The Wire*. And I'm a really good Max Bialystock in *The Producers*. But I wish I'd been *better*. Everything else I've done has pretty much been just so-so, or worse. And the more actors I get to know, the more I understand how common this low opinion of our own work is. We're a little nutty in the self-esteem department. I once worked with an *Academy Award winner* who kept saying things like, "I know you guys are wondering, 'What is this chick doing?' You're all so good. I feel like I'm dragging the whole show down. Sorry, everyone." This wasn't false modesty. She thought she sucked. In a 2003 interview with Oprah Winfrey, Julianne Moore said, "At the beginning [of a project] I'm scared. In the middle I doubt my choices. And by the end I think I've ruined it." And Meryl Streep—inarguably one of the greatest actors of our time—said she often wants to quit the week before starting a film because she thinks, "I don't know how to act. Why does anyone want to look at me on the screen anymore?" Meryl Streep, my friends.

Now if you're an actor and you're not crazy—or wildly insecure—good for you! I don't mean to suggest for one second that my assessment applies to all of us. I just think that actors, on the whole, tend to be a wee bit complicated. We think too much, we judge our work harshly, we worry constantly that we're doing something wrong, our thoughts get twisted up in knots . . . and those are the ones who've *gotten* professional help.

And then we take this already unstable group of people and subject them to a job application process that has no equal in the weird department. Other people sit down for an interview, maybe fill out an application form, take a test. Us? We take these sheets of paper with words on them, we put on a little outfit we think our character would wear, and we drive, bus, or subway to a place where we wait for our turn while others say exactly what we're about to say. Then we stand in a room with people watching us while we pretend they're not there as we read the words on the paper as if we're really saying them, as opposed to reading them, and then, if they like the way we behave as we say the words on the paper, we're invited to do the same thing for more people. If *those* people like *that* performance, we may get to do it for a larger number of people. No wonder auditioning is hard. It's an extraordinarily bizarre process.

So, to review: crazy business, crazy job description, crazy odds, very few reliable patterns, insanely short employment, crazy people, and a crazy job application process. Are we together so far?

OK. So, what's the best we can do, given all that? How do we handle the craziness, the randomness, the fact that our business is unfair, inconsistent, illogical, nonlinear, and unpredictable? What do we do?

Here's what—embrace it. Embrace the insanity of professional acting. Don't just accept it or tolerate it or slog through it. Bring yourself to *love* it, as an inherent part of this life we've chosen. And for heaven's sake, don't be surprised by it over and over again. You can't take a job at the post office and complain every day, "What's with all these letters?" That's how a post office functions. And you can't become an actor, then complain about the unfairness, injustice, or lack of security. That's the norm. That's our business doing what it does. I've seen too many actors eat themselves up inside over stuff we should fully expect as the standard course of events. Don't wrestle with the nature of this profession. You won't win. And you'll be doomed to lifelong frustration.

When someone less talented than you gets a role you wanted, remember—it's not a shocking injustice; that's showbiz. When a tremendous success is followed by months (or years) of unemployment, don't be baffled; you're in the failure business. When colleagues turn out to be a bit nutty, take it in stride; that's how actors are, generally. And if, in spite of your considerable talent, you find you're not able to make a living, remember: *nothing unusual has happened*. That's showbiz. Embrace it all. Expect it all. And as much as possible, try to develop a kind of affection for it.

Because when you sign on for the life of an actor, you don't just sign on for the days when you work and everything is nice. You sign on for the whole gestalt—the insecurity, the instability, the joy, the foolishness, the struggling, the unfairness, the fulfillment, the camaraderie—all of it. That's what this crazy life is: the whole package. No one made you sign on for this. You chose it. If you can come to love the madness, the chaos, and the wonderful, crazy unpredictability, guess what? *You _win_!*

CHAPTER TWO

INTERPRETIVE DANCE

OK. Now I'm going to hit you with a fairly big concept. I know it's only page 15 but what the hell—let's dive in. Here's a philosophical truth. Much of how we experience most of the events and circumstances we encounter in our lives is a matter of *interpretation*—how we choose to *hold* those events and circumstances in our minds. Now, obviously, there are some things that are just plain horrible, period, and some that are inarguably wonderful. But most things that happen during an average day are just things that happen—neither inherently good nor inherently bad. But then we *interpret* those events, making subconscious decisions about what they mean and how we should feel about them. We make presumptions about people's motives, and about the implications and/or consequences of what's happened. We layer all of that over (or as they say in parts of the South, "over top") the actual facts. See what I mean? All that stuff is just *interpretation*.

Nevertheless, those interpretations affect how we experience those events.

Let's say you miss your exit on the freeway. Only one thing is factual—you missed your exit. Beyond that, you could think, "Shit! Now my day is completely ruined!" Or you could think, "Oh, I'm so stupid. How could I be such an idiot?" Or you could think, "How interesting. I've never seen Cucamonga before. What an unexpected adventure." See? One event, three possible interpretations.

I want to tell you about my Aunt Joan. We used to call her "the injustice collector." She was always on the alert for ways that people were trying to screw her over. In Aunt Joan's worldview, she was at constant risk of being wronged, which made her ever vigilant against wrongdoers. Joan and I lived in the same building complex in New York City. Joan lived on the 20th floor. Again, let me emphasize those two elements of the story. New York City. 20th floor. One morning she phoned me. "Hey Joan," I said, "How are you?" "Terrible," she said. "Those maintenance bastards ran the sprinklers all night long. I didn't sleep a wink."

Now, I put it to you that the only reason my Aunt Joan, on the 20th floor, in the noisiest city this side of Tokyo, could be kept awake by *sprinklers*, for God's sake—little droplets of water falling on leaves, twenty floors below—was because of the way that she was inclined to interpret events, keeping her high-strung and hyper-defensive against these imaginary people who wanted to mess with her. The building management was simply watering the plants. Joan saw it as a secret plot to keep her awake. That's because she was looking for that. She had decided something sinister was going on and, as a result, she never got to sleep. Her actual experience was affected by how she viewed things.

Years ago, I was doing a production of Neil Simon's *Laughter on the 23rd Floor* at the Laguna Playhouse in beautiful Laguna Beach. Now, I'd done the show once before, and so, naturally, I fancied myself *quite* the expert on the piece. We had a lead who seemed unable to correctly learn his lines, and I was *appalled*. It fell to me, I decided, to defend the sanctity of the script. So I went in to see the director, Andy Barnacle, a great, upbeat guy with the irresistibly encouraging demeanor of a kids' football coach. I told him, in no uncertain terms, and with no small degree of self-righteousness, that I wasn't at all sure I wanted to do a paraphrased version of Mr. Simon's work and that I might have to leave the production.

He let me rattle on for a while. When I came up for air he gave me a smile. "Michael, let me tell you something," he said. "This is not going to be the quintessential version of *Laughter on the 23rd Floor*. But look around you. You like the condo we put you in? With the Jacuzzi tub? Have you been to the beach, just a few blocks away? You know, there's an incredible art show this time of year that you really don't want to miss. People travel for miles to see it." And then he gave me a meaningful look and added, "Enjoy your summer." And as I backed out the door I muttered something along the lines of, "Thank you very much I have no problem with that." Given circumstances: a less-than-perfect theatre job. Possible interpretations: a) artistically offensive disaster or b) a great summer in a beautiful place.

It's how I quit smoking, actually. When I first tried, I thought in terms of resisting something tempting, going without something I liked. And I kept failing, because when I craved a cigarette, I thought, "Why am I depriving myself? Screw you, world. You can't tell me what to do!" But one day, I woke up thinking, "I am not allowing those little white tubes to control my life." And every time I had a craving after that, I thought, "No. Screw you, little white tubes. I know you're trying to trick me, but I'm going to grip the handlebars and ride over this fucking cliff in flames before I let you get me." (That's what enduring the cravings felt like.) By reframing my thinking—changing my interpretation—the *temptation* was now the evil thing, trying to deprive me of clean lungs and a healthier mind. And I was determined to fight like a tiger to kick the little demon's ass.

Around now, you're probably wondering what the hell I'm on about, since we don't seem to be discussing auditioning yet. Geez, you're impatient. I promise you, there is an application of this theory to our topic. And it's simply this: if we're going to get more comfortable and have more success with auditioning, one of the things we have to do is separate solid realities from our subconscious interpretations of those realities.

When you attend an audition, the only thing that's factual is that a person or people will be performing and some other person or people will be watching. Any feelings about auditions being intimidating or nerve-wracking, about being judged or having to prove your value as an artist, about your career being on the line, are nothing but interpretations of the situation. The thing is, we're not always aware that we're adding our own spin to what's happening. And so we think our interpretations are actual facts.

I start with this because many of us view auditions with about the same terror and repulsion as we'd view a walk to the school principal's office or maybe even to the guillotine. We don't have to. There are other ways to view them. By the end of this book, one of the things I hope to convince you to do is change your interpretation of the audition experience—how you view it, how you hold it in your brain. That's a big part of what we're examining here—whether at least some of our audition problems come from our own invented versions of what's actually going on.

CHAPTER THREE

A SHOCKING PROPOSAL

O K . . . so, in acting, who gets the job? Any theories on that? Is it the actor who puts in the most time preparing? The actor with the most talent? The most training? The most impressive resumé? Is it the one who's the most attractive? The most confident? The most recognizable? The one who knows the director? The one who doesn't care about getting the part?

OK, it's a trick question. The actor who gets the job might be any of these, or none. There's no reliable, consistent pattern. We don't like that, because we're desperately looking for patterns. I've heard a dozen adamant theories over the years (including the ones above) and not one could be proven to be true in every case. Some people insist, "It's all who you know." And it *is* . . . sometimes. And sometimes it's the best actor, and sometimes it's the cutest, and sometimes we can't figure out for the life of us *why* an actor was cast. The only thing that's always true about the actor who gets hired is that somebody chose that actor.

So, OK. Put that on the back burner for now as we move on to a follow-up question: is there anything *you* can do, when you audition, to ensure that you'll get hired? Can you *become* the actor they choose for the role? If you answered no, give yourself a gold star. Of course you can't.

Yes, you should absolutely train, prepare, dress appropriately, have a great attitude, and be professional. And yes, I'd like to believe those things improve your chances. And yes, good actors work more than lousy ones, and those who are pleasant and professional work more than those who aren't.

But even if you're at your very best, perfect for the part, and delightful to work with, there's nothing you can do to *ensure* you'll be cast. The whole thing is far too random and illogical. Saying, "I'm going to go out today and book this acting job," is like saying, "I'm going to go out today and meet my future spouse." It's really not something you can control. (Trust me. It took me almost fifty years to find Mrs. Kostroff.) Friends, I'm here to tell you something you won't like but something that, on some level, you already know is true. You cannot make people cast you. You can't control their decisions. What if they want someone shorter, darker, or more like their cousin Franz? Nothing you can do. What if they deeply resent the color of your sweater? What if they lack good taste and don't recognize talent? You can't control whether you get the job simply because there are too many variables, too much subjectivity, and too little about this process that makes any sense at all.

Remind me again—*how* many times have you been brilliant at an audition and not been cast? And *how* many times have you stunk and been hired? Guess what? It's not just you. As I hope we've established by now (because it's really the cornerstone of what I'm teaching you), hiring decisions in our profession are less scientific than we'd like to believe. I know the idea isn't comfortable, but when you line up all the things we've just reviewed, the evidence is undeniable. Casting simply isn't a scientific process.

Let me tell you how unscientific casting is. A few years ago I was on the other side of the table, holding auditions for a play I was directing. This one will blow your minds: one of the actors I ended up casting was called back *by mistake*. You read that correctly. He got on the wrong list. I'd seen his initial audition and decided he wasn't quite who I was looking for. The casting director misunderstood and put him on the callback list. Too polite to cancel his appointment, I figured we'd just let him come in again and move on with our day. On second viewing, I thought, "You know, that's totally the guy." Thank God for the error. The man was brilliant in the show.

The point is, while we can *encourage* casting folks to hire us by doing a good job, the getting hired part is completely beyond our control. And it's time to make peace with that.

So, to start honoring the truth about auditioning, I'm going to propose something radical to you. You may want to sit down for this.

You should never, ever go to an audition to get a job.

"What??" you're thinking, "Madness! This book sucks! I want my money back!" Well, now, hold on. What *I* think is madness is trying to do something impossible. When you go to an audition with your focus on getting a job, you have set yourself an impossible task. Haven't you? You've chosen to focus on the thing that is the most outside of your control, and decided to try to control it. I say *that's* madness.

We've already established the undeniable mathematical reality that most of the time, we don't book the roles we audition for, because there are so many of us actors. We've agreed that when we *do* book a role, we're not always sure why. And we've admitted to ourselves that casting decisions aren't always logical, fair, smart, or artistically ideal. So going to an audition with the sole intention of getting hired kind of doesn't make a lot of sense if you think about it. Because here's the inconvenient truth: unless you possess some sort of mysterious powers that enable you to psychically intuit the desires of a person you've never met and then morph yourself to match those desires, you cannot make someone cast you. Really, the whole idea is insane.

And what's more, focusing on trying to get the job *doesn't get you the job*, does it? Hang on. Think about that for a minute. I mean honestly, how's that working out for you? Is it possible that trying to get an acting job is *not* conducive to getting an acting job? (Aha! Is that an illuminated light bulb I see over your head?) Why, yes. In fact, I believe it's completely the wrong focal point.

See? All this time you've been wondering what you've been doing wrong. You've been trying to get a job. And you really can't make that happen. No one can. No wonder you're nervous. You've been trying to do something no one knows how to do. I don't know about you, but when I try to tackle a task I don't know how to do, it makes me *really* nervous. It's as if someone had tossed you a ticking time bomb and told you to defuse it. "What do I do?!? Is it the red button or the blue button? What's this wire do? Should I smile when I meet the casting person or just start the scene? Do they want the character angry or more sarcastic?" You're trying to do something you're not equipped to do: solve an unsolvable puzzle.

And that, I believe, is where the biggest chunk of our audition anxiety comes from—trying to do the impossible, which is a nerve-wracking proposition to say the least.

But this idea is like "actor crack." We are addicted to the notion that there is some secret key that will unlock the secret formula, that there's something we can do to somehow *make* someone decide to hire us; that if we can just audition *well enough*, it'll be a done deal. We sign up for seminars and buy books that promise to reveal these magical techniques, ever hopeful that we'll somehow break the code, and from then on, it'll be smooth sailing all the way. I've spent considerable time in my workshops trying to pry people away from their obsession with this falsehood—to let go of their desperate death grip on an idea that is pure actor mythology. People have said, "But I have to get work. That's why I do this. It's not a hobby." I understand that. I'm not telling you not to want to get hired as an actor. I'm just pointing out that going to an audition and trying to get a job is *not producing your desired result*. Mostly, what it's doing is adding pressure and anxiety about the outcome of a situation you can't control. And pressure and anxiety never result in your best performance. So stop going to auditions with the purpose of getting jobs. Because most of the time—and this is just the hard, brutal, mathematical truth—you're not getting the job. Forget the damn job. It's not happening. Let it go.

Make it your new mantra: "I'm not getting the fucking job." Those are words I live by.

Because here's the thing. You're really not. Someone else is getting the job.

"But that's so negative!" I hear some earnest positive thinker object. And to that I say, oh . . . stop it. The strange times in which we live seem to be plagued by this recent, crazy-yet-popular notion that we should only say things that are "positive," whether they're true or not. I don't think it serves us to lie to ourselves. Give me reality any day, so I know what I'm dealing with.

I'm not encouraging you to be negative, just truthful. Here's the difference. If you say to yourself, "I'm probably not going to get this job, because I stink, and nothing good ever comes to me because I'm doomed," then yes, that's being negative in a way that really doesn't serve you. That's not reality. That's neurosis. Get thee to a therapist. But if you say, "I'm probably not going to get the job because, as Michael Kostroff so brilliantly points out in his brilliant book and/or workshop *Audition Psych 101*, that's the simple math of the thing. It's not any shortcoming on my part, it's just the truth of the circumstances," that's not being negative. That's being sensible. That's understanding that you and I are in the failure business, where "no sale" is the norm. My philosophy isn't some kind of mental manipulation or self-trickery. This is saying goodbye to magical thinking or the idea that you can somehow force an unlikely result. I say you're not getting the fucking job for one simple reason: you're not. I can all but guarantee it.

I want you to know that I have benefitted greatly in my career from my low expectations. I'm so clear that show business doesn't owe me a living, there's no entitlement, and that, by far, the *least* likely outcome of any audition is a job, that I get to be pleasantly shocked and amazed any time the show business gods deign to bless me with the rare gift of employment. After years of doing this, when I'm offered an acting role, I still geek out; often the first words out of my mouth are "You're *kidding!*" And that, I find, is a much more manageable way to live this life.

Now, this mantra—"You're not getting the fucking job"— may sound pretty depressing when you first hear it. But can I tell you something you may not believe? As the benefits sink in, you're going to come to love it more and more. Sit tight. We'll get there.

So . . . why even go to an audition then? Why go to the trouble of arranging your schedule, working on the dialogue, making choices about the character, planning an outfit, and traveling to a theatre or casting office? What *should* you aim for when you audition? Don't worry. I won't leave you hanging.

Many years ago, I was watching a well-known and exquisitely gifted actress on a talk show. She told a story that made an unforgettable impression on me. It was about an audition she'd been on early in her career at which she'd been incredibly nervous. You know how that is, actors? Sometimes, for some reason we'll never understand, the audition goblins get to us and we just can't seem to pull ourselves together. You know that feeling? I think most of us do. Well, she was having that kind of a day. She was at a theatre, waiting to audition, and she was a wreck. Her palms were sweating, her mind was racing, she wasn't feeling talented, and she was seriously thinking of leaving the building, and possibly the business, rather than putting herself on the line. The casting director was a friend of hers and happened to pass by the waiting area. "Oh, hey, _____," he said as he passed by, "How you doin'?" "Terrible," she spilled, "I'm nervous, I have no idea what I'm doing here, I have no ideas about the character, I'm wrong for the part, I don't feel like walking down that hallway and being judged today, and I honestly think I may just leave, because I'm really not handling this well."

The actress's casting friend gave her a smile and shrugged, "Think of it this way," he said, "It's a chance to act on a Thursday."

And this now-famous actress said that this simple little statement switched on a little light bulb in her head.

A chance to act on a Thursday. That's what you get. When you go on an audition, you're not guaranteed a job, or even a fair shot at a job. You're not guaranteed that the role is available, or that the people you're reading for will like you, or even notice you. But there's one thing you get every time you go on an audition, one thing you're *guaranteed*: a chance to act. And oh, you forgot: you *like* to act. Sometimes, when we audition, we get what I call "actors' amnesia"; we forget that we're doing something we love.

Do you know what we actors get to do the least? That's right. Act. We wait. We study. We read. We work at support jobs. We promote ourselves and our projects. We look for agents. We try to meet casting people. And once in a while, we get to do our thing. We don't get that many chances to act. When I'm working on television, do you know what the shortest part of my day is? The part when I get to actually play the character. I come in, get into makeup and wardrobe, work with the director to block the scene, then I wait while they light it. I come back in and act a little, then I wait while they move the camera and set up a new shot. Then I act a little more. And before you know it, they have what they need and they send me home. "That's it?" I think, "But . . . I hardly got to do anything!"

A chance to play a role, or sing a song, even for a few minutes, is something to be treasured. And it's a wonderful reason to audition.

Acting, as it happens, is an art form that requires an audience. You can't give a performance if you're by yourself. (Well, you can, but there are doctors who treat that type of thing.) You know when you were a kid and you put on a little show, or learned a dance, or wanted to perform a song, or do a trick, and you used to say, "Watch me! Watch me!"?

Well, today, someone is going to watch you. Someone is going to take a few minutes to watch you do what you love doing. How 'bout that? Isn't that so neat?

It is a wondrous thing to have the opportunity to perform and have folks watch you. During those few moments, you are fulfilling your calling (if you believe in such things, as I do). At that instant, you are an actor. You're doing what actors do—playing a character, telling a story, replicating behavior, attempting that magic trick in which the false appears real. It's all the things that made you want to perform in the first place. If you forget about the fucking job—take away the joy-killing task of trying to get employed and remember that you like acting—the whole experience may start to change; it can be a heavenly, fulfilling, satisfying endeavor, just like when you're on stage or on set.

When I lived in LA, I got accustomed to driving around to various studios for auditions. My agent would call with an appointment and off I'd go. I got used to it. It was something I did countless times—so many times, in fact, that after a while, it became routine. But this one day, for some reason, it suddenly struck me. I remember that I was in the left lane, about to turn onto the lot at Paramount Studios in Hollywood. Now Paramount is the one that has those huge, beautiful, ornate gates. It's the studio entrance you see in *Sunset Boulevard* and it's one of the most iconic images of Hollywood's Golden Age. And this particular day I suddenly thought, "Wait a minute! Let's just assess here. Here's what's happening. I'm about to make a left turn and drive through those gates. And when I get to the guard shack, I'm going to tell the guard my name, and he's going to check his computer, and *my name is going to be there*! They're expecting me! Someone at Paramount Studios has asked me to come audition for a professional television show. They want to see me! Hang on . . . that's badass!" And I remembered that there was a time I didn't have opportunities like the ones I'd been taking for granted. And I remembered what a privilege it was to be a professional actor, invited to audition, and what a joy it was to get to act that afternoon.

You don't need to be driving onto the lot of a big Hollywood movie studio to appreciate how cool it is to be an actor. You just have to stop and take note of where you are—as you step onto a stage, as you elevator up to a casting office, as you warm up for a dance call, as you sign in for a commercial audition—and remind yourself that you're doing the thing you wanted to do. Just by auditioning, you're doing what actors do. You're being an actor.

So now, you have a new reason and a new focus when you go to an audition. Go, because today, you get to do what you love for a few minutes. It's a chance to act on a Thursday. And that's a terrific thing for us lunatics who like stepping into other characters. We love this stuff!

Now, question: if, when you audition, your only satisfactory outcome is getting a job, how often will you be disappointed? That's right. All the bloody time. But if you make it your goal to simply do what actors do and play a role for a few minutes while people watch, how often do you get what you came for? That's right. Every single time. Every time you go in with the plan to simply do your work as an actor and play a scene, and you complete that task, you get to ring the bell—assignment fulfilled. Check the box. Forget about whether or not you feel it went well. There's no self-evaluation in this assignment. This new goal is to simply show up and do your work.

And take a look at this. Once you embrace the fact that you're not getting the fucking job, the pressure is suddenly off. If you know you're not getting the job, what is there to worry about? You don't have to get it right, make an impression, do it better than anyone else, or anything. There's nothing on the line. You're not getting it. So you're free to play the character the way you see it. (Yes—of course—you want to read the character description and make use of any guidelines that are provided and any direction you're given. But beyond that, you get to just come in and do your thing.)

For years, the folks who cast *Les Misérables* kept calling me in to audition for the deliciously desirable role of Thenardiér, the comically evil innkeeper who sings "Master of the House." They auditioned me and auditioned me, and continued to not cast me. Every six months or so, I'd get another call from my agent: "They want to see you again." At one point they said, "We're so sorry we keep dragging you in here. We like you. We just don't have a spot for you." "You never have to apologize for calling me in," I assured them, "Because every time I'm here, I'm the only Thenardiér in the room. None of you get to be Thénardier. Just me. I get to play this role for a few minutes, and it's a really good role. So call me in any time you like." And they continued to do just that. It wasn't a tactic. I meant it. I was enjoying the only guarantee I had—this great opportunity to play the conniving, bombastic, filthy Thenardiér on a Thursday.

You don't have the job. The cold, mathematical, all-but-guaranteed likelihood is that you're not going to get the job. But you do have the role . . . for about three minutes. While you're in there, you're the only one playing that character. Relish your work. Do what you do. And for God's sake, don't miss it! It's over before you know it.

Over the next several chapters, we're going to go through the audition process together, putting each phase under a microscope, from the moment the audition is scheduled until the moment the job is booked (by someone else), and see if we can fix some of the places where we get weird and some of the faulty ideas we have about this stuff.

Now, just so you know, I'm going to be repeating our new mantra a lot. I don't do that to be annoying. It's just that I find, even after years of teaching this stuff, that I have to keep reminding myself, "Michael, you're not getting the fucking job. What are you even worrying about?" In the heat of the moment, in the excitement over an audition opportunity, it's easy to fall off the wagon. Believe me, you'll thank me later.

CHAPTER FOUR

PREPARE YOURSELF

O K. You have an upcoming audition. Maybe it's an open call you read about online, or maybe an agent has gotten you an appointment. Doesn't matter; we're just pretending. The first thing most of us do is get very happy and excited. The second thing most of us do is freak out. We look at the audition materials and we think, "Damn it! I have no idea how to do this! I don't have a take on this role at all! There's hardly any information! There isn't enough time! This sucks! Why me?" As soon as the audition becomes specific—a specific character in a specific project—many of us short circuit. (I myself have occasionally been heard to whine, "I *hate* acting!" when faced with real words on a real page.)

And there it is. Before we've even begun the work of preparing, we've hit a psychological bump. Not to worry. This is totally normal. Actors at all levels pass through this tunnel of despair. But when it happens, it's helpful to recognize that you're just being a little neurotic, because that understanding will help make these meltdowns as brief as possible. All that stuff does is delay the work. If you're an actor, this is the task you're born for—you take words on a page and turn them into characterizations. You know how to do this. You've just forgotten for the moment that you know how to do it. So stop flailing about, take a deep breath, and get to work.

Now, how do we approach that work? Many actors, when preparing to audition, start by trying to figure out the answer to the age-old question, "What do they want?" I want you to mentally draw a big fat line through those words and never ask "What do they want?" again. Because, once again, you're presenting yourself with an unsolvable puzzle. You'll never be able to guess what they want, they sometimes don't know what they want, and each casting director has different tastes. And even if you *did* know what they wanted, you couldn't become that. See what an impossible predicament you're putting yourself in when you try to guess what "they" want?

What if we remove the whole idea of preparing what we think "they" want (I mean, beyond what's written in the character description)? Just throw that idea out entirely. What if we, knowing as we now do, that we're not going to get the fucking job, and that we only have the role for a few minutes, go in there and play it the way *we* want to? What if we just go in and present *our* take on the material? Because ultimately, that's all you have. Is it "right"? Who knows? Who cares? You're not getting the fucking job. Go do your thing.

And since this is the only time you'll be playing this part, approach the preparation the same way you'd approach a role you'd booked. Don't wait, thinking you'll do the work once you've landed the job. You're not going to get that chance. This is it. Now's the time to look up words and references you don't know, and to do all the stuff you learned in acting class: figure out what your character wants, your objectives, the obstacles, the stakes, the circumstances, the physicality, the voice. Remember that your work is incomplete until you understand what happens *between* the lines, when *other* characters are speaking. Don't go dead just because you're not talking. Decide how you feel about what you're *hearing*. Play the whole scene. I don't understand why we treat auditions like something other than acting, why we give in to the temptation to fashion superficial line readings and expressions (what I call "audition acting") rather than getting to the truth of our work.

I have learned, over years of coaching other actors for their auditions, that the best way to banish nerves and anxieties is to invest deeply in the work itself. Ask yourself a lot of questions, working to understand your character's point of view. Want something in the scene. And try to get it. Make it important.

Remember, the role is all yours for about three minutes. So play it. Perform the hell out of it. Relish the opportunity to do what you love. And do it the way that *you* feel it should be done. That's the performance to prepare. It's all yours. Don't audition for it. Play it.

Now, there's a psychological benefit to making the pages your own. According to your taste, circle, box, or highlight your lines, make notes in the margins, mark things up—whatever works for you. What some actors do—me included—is retype the whole thing, with their characters' lines in a larger font or in bold so it's easier to find one's place during the reading. Others like to eliminate the stage directions. It doesn't matter what your preferences are. The point is, take ownership. Before you got the materials, they belonged to the casting people. Now they're yours. Reworking them for yourself helps you feel like the expert you are, completely in control of the decisions about your work and how to do it. This kind of interaction with the material also helps you memorize.

And that's the other thing you're going to do, since this is the only time you're playing this part: memorize your lines. Of course you do. Why wouldn't you? Don't you always memorize lines when playing a role? Memorizing deepens your understanding of the character and gets your eyes off the page so you can really play the scene. And watching you interact with your scene partner will always be more interesting than watching the top of your head.

By the way, as a side note, even if you have the lines down cold, always hold the sides or script while auditioning. If you don't, the casting director may start to focus on how well you've learned the lines and miss out on your performance. It becomes a memorization test, and that could make him nervous. (Have you ever placed an order with a waiter who refused to write it down? I don't know about you, but I start to focus on that and it makes me a little nervous. And about 20% of the time, what comes to the table isn't what I ordered, and I wish he'd written it down instead of showing off.) The other reason to hold the pages is that it subconsciously reminds the people watching that the material is new to you and they're not seeing a final product. You're open to notes and direction. "You like me now? This is just what I've done on my own."

Figure out your character's job in the story. This is an important consideration many actors miss. I built my TV resumé by starting with a string of very small roles—one or two lines. Here's the trick when auditioning for those: don't do too much. Imagine watching the final product, and think about what you'd expect to see from this small character. Think about what best facilitates the overall story—what your character's job is and, more importantly, what it is not. If you're going in for the role of a waitress, and your line is "More coffee?" the writer most likely did not intend for audience members to have lingering questions about her emotional state or personal history. "I wonder what was going on with that waitress. She seemed troubled when she asked if they wanted more coffee. And I felt like she had a history with the man at the table. I'll bet we're going to see more of her. There was something going on there." If the audience reacts like that, the waitress has failed to fulfill her job in the story by doing way too much with her one line. It's also a mistake to make "creative" choices for the sole purpose of standing out. If the story takes place in Ohio and you decide your character has a cockney accent, it creates random intrigue and confusion that would distract from an audience's focus on the actual story.

I once went in for a role on *Dharma and Greg* of a cop with one line—just three words. The exchange went something like this:

> Cop 1 (not me): You know, I don't think we've ever arrested anyone for doing it on the steps of the capital. Hey Lou, have we ever arrested anyone for doing it on the steps of the capital?
>
> Lou (me): Don't think so.

Now, I knew that many of my fellow character men were coming in with quirky, "creative" choices, showing Lou's thought process and demonstrating their wacky sitcom charm, and I sensed that would be way too much for Lou. So I went to the audition with a crossword puzzle[2], barely acknowledged anyone in the room, and sat there working on it. When the reader gave the cue line, I mumbled, "Don't think so," without even looking up. I got cast, and I think it was partially because I understood Lou's job in the story. That was really all the audience needed from Lou.[3]

Auditions for one- and two-line parts aren't your opportunities to demonstrate your full range of ability. Sometimes, the best thing is to just say the damn words with no "spin." When preparing, make choices that facilitate the *storytelling*, not your desire to shine. That's thinking like an actor, not an auditioner.

---

[2] Generally speaking, don't use props. You don't need them. I broke my own rule on this one.

[3] In order to make my point, I had to admit to getting cast as Lou. But now, please forget that I told you that part. This never happens.

Now, obviously, the same consideration applies to larger roles. If you're auditioning for *A Funny Thing Happened on the Way to the Forum* and you're reading for any character *other* than Pseudolous, part of your job is to be gullible enough to be fooled by him. If you play your character as wise, knowing, and savvy, you can ruin the whole story. If you're auditioning to play Juliet but decide to play it like she's only mildly interested in Romeo, the whole plot falls apart. So know your job. Is your character there to scare the others? To show the main character's bad luck with dating? To be the butt of the joke? To establish the location? To inspire the hero? Be sure you understand what your purpose is and how you fit into the plot.

If you find yourself thinking about how to stand out, be interesting, or make an impression, you're already headed down the wrong path. Those goals can lead to strange, desperate choices, as opposed to just plain good acting. If you decide, for no reason, to give the computer programmer you're playing a French accent and a limp, trust me, you'll stand out all right. But not in a good way.

And this is also why you want to read the whole script if it's available, or watch the movie, if there is one (as there sometimes is when you're auditioning for theatre), or watch an episode of the TV show you're reading for. These things may help you understand the tone and the context of your audition material, which will make you feel more solid going in. Plus, as research goes, reading plays or watching TV isn't exactly grueling.

Now, I know how we are; we get obsessive, so let me back you away from the edge here. This research isn't *crucial*, it's just helpful. If you don't have the time, or can't get the script, please don't panic. Nothing is ruined. Remember, there are not a lot of patterns in our business. So it's not as if the person who doesn't do this type of research is dead in the water. I just find I feel more satisfied with my work, and hence my audition experience, when I delve a bit. (Full disclosure: if I'm busy, I read only the stuff my character is in, because he wouldn't usually be aware of things happening in other scenes.)

Next, very important: you must always, always go over the material out loud, with someone else. If you can, hire an audition coach. Can't afford one? Can't find one? That's OK. Get a fellow actor to run over everything with you. If you prefer, you can ask your friend not to give notes or direct you. Just run the words a few times. But one way or another, you should always do it *out loud, with someone*. The reason you do that is this: you don't want to be standing in front of the casting director the first time those words come out of your mouth. I have, several times, ignored my own advice and gone in without running the dialogue with anyone (because I'm such an "expert," you see) and found myself in the middle of the audition, having just spoken a line, realizing, "Oh . . . that's what that meant." And by then it's too late. When you read the lines, out loud, with someone, you make discoveries; some of those discoveries are questions that lead to other discoveries. For some reason, no matter how much you can discover while reading the lines by yourself, saying them *out loud, with someone* sheds even more light and makes things make better sense.

It also gets the "lousy read" out of the way. The first few times through, the lines never come out the way you heard them in your head and the performance usually just stinks. So get that version out of the way with someone who isn't the casting person.

Deciding what to wear to your audition is another part of your preparation. Here's my rule of thumb. Wear something that helps the casting person see the character, but *don't* wear a costume. If you're going in for the role of Brutus, wear a loose-fitting shirt but not a toga. A full costume reads as desperate and makes people uncomfortable; you're not applying for a job in wardrobe. On the other hand, if you wear a tailored business suit to audition for the role of a small-town farm girl, it confuses people and doesn't help you feel the part. Wear something that gives the vibe of the character—a suit for a lawyer, khakis for a soldier, a sundress for a hippie, jeans and a tee shirt for a rock singer. Pay attention to colors and the ideas they evoke. The sweet, befuddled science professor might be more likely to wear tweedy browns than icy gray pinstripe. The party planner can probably pull off the vibrant purple scarf, while the repressed romance novelist might be better served by the faded pink sweater. Never let your outfit be the star. Think of it more like a supporting player.

And now, we interrupt this chapter for an important public service announcement. Here, I must caution you all about a dreaded condition that runs rampant among the acting community, one to which actors preparing for auditions are particularly susceptible. It's called The Upfers. Symptoms of The Upfers are easy to detect. When you hear yourself telling people, "I'm up for this part on *Law & Order: SVU*." . . . "I'm up for the role of Sarah in *Ragtime*." . . . "I'm up for a Doritos commercial." I'm up for this; I'm up for that—you've got The Upfers.

Actors, don't talk about your auditions. Keep them to yourself.

Now, why would I say that? Why would I advise you not to tell anyone about your auditions? Well, let's review. How often do you get the roles you audition for? Correct—almost never. So that means that if you tell people about everything you're up for, you're going to spend a lot of time explaining about jobs you didn't get.

"Hey what ever happened to that role you were up for?"
"Oh . . . I didn't get it."
"Hey, didn't you go in for that national tour?"
"Oh . . . yeah . . . I didn't get it."
"Hey, I saw that Doritos commercial. Where were you?"
"I wasn't in it. I didn't get it."

Didn't get it. Didn't get it. That's the message you're sending out to colleagues—which isn't great for your reputation—and to yourself—which isn't great for your self-esteem. Again and again, you're listening to yourself say, "I didn't get it," and you start to feel like a failure, when in reality, not getting a role is the *norm*! Don't do that to yourself. When you go in for a role—which, I promise you, you're not going to get—don't tell anyone. You're stirring an empty pot.

And you *especially* don't want to tell civilians (non-showbiz folk or, as one of my students called them, "Muggles"[4]). Because they *really* don't get how things work. Your aunt Martha in Iowa will want to know *why*. "Well, honey, what happened? I can't imagine why they wouldn't cast you! Did you tell them you played a doctor in the high school play? Did you tell them you're very interested and could start immediately? You have to assert yourself, honey, or you'll never get anywhere in this world." And then, on top of your own disappointment, you have to deal with Aunt Martha's.

You got a callback? Congratulations. Now you *really* need to stay tight-lipped. What do you need with the pressure of people asking for details when you're trying to stay focused on your work? Invariably, they call or text to ask, "How did it go?" when you haven't even gone in yet, and it just adds weight to the thing.

You've been told that the project is a definite go? Or that the role is yours, but the director just needs to meet you as a formality? Or that an offer is coming? Keep it to yourself. Do you know how many so-called "definites" never come to pass? As I always say, in our business, nothing is anything until it's something.

Now, I have a reputation as an actor who works all the time. "That fuckin' Kostroff. Works all the time." Someone once said to me, "Geez! You walk into a Starbucks and someone gives you a job!" Nonsense. I don't work all the time. Want

----

[4] "Muggles" are what the non-magical people are called in the *Harry Potter* series of books and films.

to know why I have that reputation? Because I don't believe in discussing auditions, so no one ever hears about the acting jobs I don't book. All they see is me working. And that's a whole lot better for my self-esteem than sharing every damn thing I audition for.

I'm often asked this, so let me anticipate a question here: "So, when people ask what I'm up to, what should I say? Can't I be proud of what's happening in my career?" Well, yes, of course you can, but if someone asks what you're doing, and you say, "I'm up for a role," that doesn't really say anything. It's not an indication of success and really, it's not even noteworthy. Auditioning is all in a day's work for an actor. As someone brilliantly said in one of my workshops, "I work as a bartender. I don't tell people every time I make a Cosmo."

Here's some food for thought: aren't there other things to talk about? I've gotten so sick of hearing the same conversation from actors again and again: "I had an audition," "I can't seem to get an audition," "I need an agent," "I got an agent," "Things are slow," et cetera. If someone asks what you're up to, why not tell them about something you've read, or a fun visit with your family, or your obsession with a new game, or your plans to go to a friend's wedding? Much more fun, and much less typical!

Or, you could use the trick one of my friends uses: "I have something in the works I'm not allowed to talk about. We should know by the end of the week." I think that's pretty transparent, but if you can pull it off with a straight face, God bless you.

I know it's exciting to have an audition, but I think you'll find that *not* discussing them helps you audition better. Ultimately, it's a solitary undertaking; you walk in alone. No number of well-wishers can help you do this work, and too much chatter can distract you. It's between you, the material, and the casting person. Work thoughtfully, privately, and secretly.

And finally, as part of your preparation, start looking forward to your auditions. There's no reason they can't be completely enjoyable. Remember, I say that as someone who used to dread them, so you can trust what I'm telling you.

CHAPTER FIVE

THE WAITING ROOM: CHAMBER OF DREAD

O K, so you've gotten your appointment, you've worked on your materials, gone over them with a friend or coach, figured out your character's job in the story, and planned what to wear. Now it's the day of the audition, and you must travel to a designated location where you will enter the Chamber of Dread, the waiting room. And it is here, I believe, that most of us do most of our falling apart. Here, in the waiting room, lie the greatest opportunities for self-sabotage and disabling anxiety.

I don't know if this happens to anyone else. My first thought when I walk through the door to a waiting room is always, "There are others?" Somehow, in my preparation, I forget that I'm not the only person auditioning for the role. It surprises me every damn time. And then the next thing I usually do is mentally cast someone else, thinking, "Oh, he's perfect. He's definitely got it. That's who I'd cast. Why are the rest of us even here?"

And then I sit down. And I wait.

And what makes the waiting room particularly treacherous is that they're almost always running late. Almost always. And so you wait.

And you wait.

And . . . you wait.

And as the clock ticks, your mind may descend into madness, and begin to resemble a Dali painting, all melted and twisted and weird. And that's when you begin to wonder, as you sit there, why you picked this stupid shirt . . . and whether you might have the completely wrong take on the role . . . and you start to think about quitting the business . . . and you decide that everyone else is more experienced than you are, and that you're not only a huge phony but the only phony there—a no-talent fake in a room full of *real* actors.

And that's usually when they call your name.

I'm going to help you. I'm going to arm you with a bunch of tools for surviving the dreaded waiting room. Try them out and discover which ones help you battle your particular entourage of gremlins. And for Pete's sake, write them on your index card.

But first, I'm going to tell you something I think you'll find surprising. When you see actors whose work you know, it's tempting to think they have it made and that they must have great self-esteem. I'm here to tell you, it's not true. It doesn't feel all that different, being a working actor with major credits. At least not to me. So if you see one of us in the waiting room, don't be intimidated. If we're there, it means we're auditioning, just like you, and just like you, we're putting ourselves on the line.

Now here are those tools I promised you.

- Stop cramming. By "cramming," I mean frantic, last-minute studying and reviewing of your materials. No one ever becomes a much better performer in the five minutes before walking through the door to the casting office. You will not be getting some brand-new, last-minute epiphany that will make the scene suddenly all make sense to you. In our saner moments, we know this. And yet, if you look around a waiting room, you'll see actors manically reading their materials over and over and over again, desperately glued to those pages, afraid to break their gaze for one second, as if something might jump out of the paper at any moment and slap them in the face, giving them the magical reading that's going to book the job. They review their music again and again, petrified that one moment away from it will result in certain disaster as they madly vocalize to make sure the notes are still there. That's nuts, people. Put the pages down. Stop vocalizing. Work on things like relaxing and getting into character. Stop cramming. All that does is stir up your anxiety and send you a subconscious message that you're not ready to audition. I'm not saying you can't look at the materials at all. If you want to look them over a time or two and remind yourself what the scene is, that's fine. But don't be weird. Trust that you've done your work, and let it go. That will do more to positively affect your state of mind than any amount of reviewing.

- Don't feel stuck to your chair. No one has ordered you to sit still and not speak or move. You're not being punished. Get up, move around, loosen up, or, even better . . .

- Take a fucking walk. For God's sake, take a walk. If you know it's going to be a while before you go in to audition, then get out of that weird, waiting-room atmosphere, stretch your legs, stroll the hallways, or go outside and get some air, and think about how cool it is that you're about to act for a few minutes. Just be sure not to miss your turn.

- Review your index card. Remember how I told you to write down reminders for yourself? Now's the time when they'll have the most value.

- Avoid the waiting room "energy suckers." You know the people I mean. I'll bet many of you reading this book can recall specific incidents when you found yourself in the presence of an energy sucker. These are other actors whose behavior makes it tough to maintain your pre-audition equilibrium like, for example, those who might want to converse a lot when you're trying to prepare, or who are so nervous that their weird energy fills the waiting room, affecting everyone. Sometimes they're jaded, embittered actors who sit there bitching about everything. Or, sometimes—I'm sorry to say it but it's true—sometimes, they're petty, conniving competitors who want to psych you out. Don't get stuck in a conversation you don't want to have—or overhearing a conversation you don't want to overhear.

If an energy sucker is talking to you, it can be hard to extricate yourself—we're all so damned *nice*. We don't want to hurt anyone's feelings. So I've figured out a way to handle that situation. It's silly, but it works. Behave as if you've misunderstood the conversation to be over. Just interrupt immediately and say, as you walk away, "Great! That's so cool. Oh my God, we have to catch up! You look amazing! Knock 'em dead in there!" and keep moving. Don't wait for them to release you or stop talking (it's possible they never will). Boldly interrupt in a friendly, upbeat way and *walk away*. Energy sucker: "But wait, I wanted to ask you something!" You (with a friendly chuckle, as if you didn't hear): "Oh, I know! See you later. Go get this job, willya?" And if that doesn't work, then you really do need to be clear and firm, even if someone gets miffed. You don't want to be thinking on the ride home, "Ugh! I let that idiot ruin my audition experience!"

If someone is being loud or distracting, I find a smile always softens a request. So instead of crab-bily complaining, "Excuse me, could you hold it down? You're not in your living room," you could smile warmly and say something like, "Hi. So sorry to interrupt, but I have terrible concentration and I'm trying to prepare. Would it be possible for you to talk outside?" And if they say no, just smile and say, "No worries. I just had to ask." That usually gets them to at least quiet down.

As an alternative, earbuds or headphones can be your best friends. Those things are gifts from God, sent down from heaven especially for performers in waiting rooms. I know actors who program a playlist for each audition to help put themselves in the right frame of mind. I think that's kind of bril-liant. But even with nothing playing, having those things in your ears can do a lot to keep people from bothering you and throwing you off.

Of course, you also have to make sure not to *be* an energy sucker. If you're doing anything in the wait-ing room that distracts other actors from their work, then you're not doing yours effectively.

- Read . . . *something other than your sides!* Oh my God! Radical! But if you put the script down and read something else (I can recommend a fun little book called *Letters from Backstage* by some guy called Michael Kostroff), you start to think, "Wow. I must really be calm. Look at me, reading something *else*.

I guess I'm ready for this audition." You're sending yourself a subconscious message that everything is OK. And really, everything *is* OK.

Plus, when people see you reading something other than the script, it really fucks with their minds. I'm KIDDING!

- OK. This is going to sound all noble and spiritual, but it's not. You really want to calm yourself down? I promise, this works. Look around the waiting room at all the other actors, and think about them, and in your heart, wish them well. One by one, send good thoughts. Maybe *they're* nervous. Wish them well. Not out loud. Just in your heart. If you're a praying person, pray—*not for yourself.* Pray for the others. Now, why do I tell you not to pray for your own audition? I'll tell you why . . . and I'm not trying to interfere in your spiritual life. Praying for your own audition can be another thing that whips up your nerves and frantic energy. "Oh, God PLEASE let me do well. I just HAVE to get this job. Lord I'm so nervous. HELP ME! OH, GOD. *PLEASE* GOD!" See what I mean? Do yourself a favor. Pray for someone else.

Believe it or not, there was one young woman in one of my classes who objected to this last suggestion. "I'm not going to pray for someone else! They're my competition!" she said. And that made my brain twist up into knots. Hang on a second, I thought, you really think you're that powerful? You really think God is going to say, "Well, OK. I was going to give the part to you, but seeing as how you prayed for the others, I'll give it to one of them. Nice going, dummy." That's some mighty strange religion. You honestly believe that being mentally stingy toward your colleagues improves your chances, and that praying for someone else's audition will take a job away from you? That's loony. You know what it'll take away? Your nerves!

- Think about what's next in your day. And there should always be something next. "Let's see, what am I doing after the audition? Oh, right. I'm headed to the store for groceries, then to meet Phil and see that play." It reminds you that life will continue after you do the scene, or sing the song, and that auditioning isn't the only thing happening in the world.

- You want to know what else you can do while waiting to audition? You may want to brace yourself; this is pretty crazy. You could do your *acting preparation for the scene you'll be performing*. <u>What?</u> Heresy! You know, I marvel that this seems to be the last thing we think of doing. You have all this time in the waiting room. You could work on getting into the character's frame of mind and reflect on what the piece is about. Think of it as your dressing room or trailer, and do the work you do when you're about to perform. Just do it in your head, so you don't bother anyone.

Now, this isn't a book on acting technique, so I leave it to you to discover your own methodology through that kind of study. But, for example, if you're using sense memory, why not start creating those sensations in the waiting room? If you're a "what if" kind of actor like me, mentally put yourself in the character's environment and circumstances. I'll sometimes wander the halls or walk around outside, imagining what I'd see, hear, and so forth, if I were the character. For example, if I'm auditioning to play a grocery store manager, I'll walk around picturing the food on the shelves, feeling the cold of the air conditioning, hearing the music and conversations, smelling the smells. All this, mind you, in lieu of sitting there, nervously staring at the paper. Doesn't that sound like more fun? If it's a highly emotional scene, you might silently work on creating that internal emotional state. This way, when you walk through the door to audition, you've already got your motor going, so to speak.

I always get asked this, so I'll include it here. "But what if I'm doing this big emotional scene and I get myself all ready and I go in and they want to chit chat?" OK, Mr. Worry-Pants. I have an answer for you. Do your preparation, then put the character's emotional state on the back burner so you can act like a normal person when you walk through the door and greet the casting person. The preparation will still be there. Just put it aside for a moment.

That said, you can also grow some actor balls and say what you need . . . nicely. "Let's talk after the scene. It's kind of big and emotional and I'd love to just dive right into it." You might be surprised how often that kind of clarity will be honored and respected.

- Reclaim the feeling of being in control. One of the things that fosters waiting-room terror is the feeling that we're trapped—our fates are sealed—no turning back—no choice in the matter. As they call the name of each actor ahead of us on the list, it can feel as though we're being pushed, inch by inch, toward the edge of a cliff by a big, slow-moving bulldozer, with no way to escape the impending fall into the abyss. Right? Of course, right. You think I don't know that feeling? I've had that feeling plenty. So here's what I want you to do. This sounds dopey. Do it anyway. Remind yourself that if you wanted to, you could leave. The door is right there. You have the physical ability to get to it. No one would stop you. And very likely, no one would care. Remind yourself that you have the option of walking out and give yourself complete permission to do so. Most likely, if you really give yourself a choice, you'll decide to stay. But this tiny mental practice makes a world of difference. I've sometimes thought to myself, "Geez, Michael, you're really nervous! Do you want to just . . . go?" And I really consider that option for a moment, and then I think, "No, I think I'll stay. Yeah. I'll stay. Why not?" I've now *decided* that I *want* to audition. Suddenly, no one is forcing me. No bulldozer. No cliff.

- Decide to look forward to going into the audition room. Look at the door, and think, "Cool! In just a few moments, I get to walk through that door into that other room and people are going to watch me do what I love. Neat!" As you hear the other actors' names called, think, "Lucky! They get to go in now. I can hardly wait!" Remember, your ideas about what lies on the other side of that door often suffer from interpretation. You're not about to have surgery. You're not going before a firing squad or a grand jury. No one is going to hit you or yell at you. You're going in to meet with someone who is rooting for you. And you get to be an actor!

- Remember the unnamed famous actress: it's a chance to act on a Thursday!

- Here's a suggestion from Gordon Hunt's book *How to Audition*. Think about the fact that somewhere near you, there's a hospital. And within the walls of that hospital, some very important milestones are taking place; someone is being born and someone else is passing out of this life. All around you, and all around the world, things are happening *in this very moment* that are much more important than whether you book three lines as a dancing pepperoni in a pizza commercial. In a universal sense, your audition is miniscule.

This story may or may not be true, but it's what I heard, and I hope it is. On opening night of each of his shows, the famous theatrical impresario Gower

Champion used to send every member of the cast the same telegram. Every actor in every show he did. Same exact message. And that message was:

JUST REMEMBER (STOP) ONE BILLION CHINAMEN [5]
DON'T GIVE A FUCK WHAT HAPPENS TONIGHT (STOP)

When we're in the waiting room, it's easy to let what's about to happen grow in size and importance until it takes up the whole universe. It's like a huge, flaming ball that blocks our view of everything else. But trust me, there's some farmer in a field in Bolivia who doesn't really give a shit. He's got his own problems. Oh yeah, and then there's stuff like poverty and global warming and missing kids and I could go on, but you get the picture. Think about all this, and your audition is suddenly not such a big deal.

- Consider that this audition isn't the top of the mountain for you. It's not the ultimate goal of your career. I made this discovery while waiting to audition for a recurring role on *The Geena Davis Show*. I'd never been called back for a recurring role before and I was a little nervous. And I heard myself thinking, "Oh, if I could just get this part. Imagine what that would do for my career. I just want to get this job!" But then I thought, "Wait a minute. I don't

---

[5] I urge you not to take offense at the use of this less-than-politically-correct racial identifier. As I heard it, this was the word Mr. Champion used, which, given the time period, is likely to be true.

just want this job. I don't just want a recurring role on *The Geena Davis Show*, for heaven's sake! I plan on doing plenty of recurring roles in my career, and guest starring roles, and one day, I want to star in *The Michael Kostroff Show*. Of course I can handle this one. It's just the first of many—a stepping-stone along the path of my career." After thinking that, the audition suddenly felt like small potatoes. (I always liked that expression. What the hell does it mean?) "Aw, this audition is nothing in the big picture," I thought, "One of hundreds." And my nerves vanished. Recognizing that this particular audition isn't the Holy Grail or the end of the rainbow might help you, as it did me, to relax and present your work.

CHAPTER SIX

ON DIGNITY

While we're waiting in the waiting room, let's have a little sidebar. I'd like to talk about a subject that I don't think actors reflect on nearly enough: the subject of dignity.

It's not always easy to feel dignified as an actor. Indeed, I think most of us would agree that there are many elements of our profession that can pose challenges to our sense of dignity. For one thing, there are so, so many of us. It's very hard to feel special. Also, some of the situations in which we find ourselves can feel less than dignified. Not everyone respects actors; some even mistreat us. And sometimes, there's a sense that we're at the mercy of those who hold the power. Some actors say they feel they have to endure whatever is thrown at them. And there's not much dignity in that.

And yet, I believe that a sense of personal dignity is a crucial part of what we bring into a room. This profession doesn't hand that to us, and so it falls to each of us to cultivate and nurture and sustain that dignity for ourselves, no matter how many forces are working against it.

Most of us know lots and lots of actors, and many of us live in cities where there are thousands of us, which makes it easy to forget this, so let me remind you: not everyone can do what we do. It is a magic trick, this morphing into other people, making someone else's words sound like ours, making the false appear real. Don't you know how amazing that is? We are marvelous, mysterious creatures, we actors. And I think it's important not to allow our vast numbers, or the occasional disrespect we encounter, to separate us from that awareness.

Remember, before there were agents, casting directors, or artistic directors, there were actors. We started this stuff. The middlemen joined in later, and now they call many of the shots. Still, we're the ones who do the actual magic. We are practitioners of an ancient, mystical art, and as such, we are worthy of dignity.

A few years back, my wife and I went to see a Broadway revival of *Cyrano*. Before the show, a family sat down directly in front of us—father, mother, a little girl of about 9, and a little boy of about 13. At first, we were concerned they'd talk and fidget and cause distraction. But the four of them sat there, in rapt silence, for the entire play. When the houselights came up at the end, my wife and I (already misty-eyed) were moved to see that the little girl had one little tear running down her cheek. But what really choked us up was noticing the boy, who wasn't ready to leave his seat. His father spoke to him gently but the boy protested, "It's not fair. It's not fair that Cyrano doesn't get to be with Roxanne. He loved her so much! That can't be the end! He loved her!" My wife and I just started weeping. She turned to me and whispered, "I love what you do." And it occurred to me that all we'd seen was just some lights, some pieces of scenery, and some actors, speaking words. It's because of them that this little boy was so affected that he couldn't leave the theatre.

The late legendary acting teacher Milton Katselas said:

> I think that the most important thing for an actor is dignity—that an actor has a sense of dignity. And by dignity, I don't mean pride, I don't mean false hope. I don't mean hostility. I mean a sense of the fact that he is in . . . one of the most highly-thought-of professions in the history of man. Perhaps one has difficulty getting a credit card—but it's not that kind of dignity that I'm talking about. Each and every person that has ever attended any theatrical or movie adventure . . . has gotten some kind of information that they've been able to apply to their lives . . . And the actor is the source of that. *And therefore, when an actor goes on an interview, he doesn't have to be a beggar . . .* saying, "I've got to have this," no matter how broke

he is. He must be willing to be himself at that interview: Not to fake, not to pretend, and not to try to sell a big thing, but to be himself, and to come with a certain dignity, and not to be talked out of that dignity . . . If the actor handles himself with dignity, and with presence . . . he *cannot lose*, because if it's not this thing, then it will be something else . . . You have got to win—*you cannot lose if you come that way.*[6]

Those are thoughts worth chewing on.

The brilliant Albert Hague was a Broadway composer (*Redhead, Plain and Fancy*) who went on to play "Mr. Shorofsky" in the film *Fame* as well as on the TV series that followed. He also used to teach an audition class that I had the privilege of attending.

Albert Hague had some radical ideas about auditioning and about self-esteem. I want to share some of those ideas with you because they're worth trying on for size. I don't advocate that you follow these, necessarily. I just want you to read them and realize that you have choices, and authority, and value.

Hague suggests that we never allow anyone to keep us waiting more than a half hour. After thirty minutes, Hague says, get up, gather your things, and graciously tell the monitor

---

[6] Quoted from an interview in *How to Audition* by Gordon Hunt. Used with permission. (italics mine)

or casting assistant, "I'm terribly sorry. I won't be able to wait any longer. I have another appointment." Often, he says, the assistant will ask you to wait just a moment while she talks to the people in the room. When she returns, she'll likely say, "They can see you next if you can wait another few minutes," an offer you magnanimously accept. And now, when you go in, you have their full attention, because they're thinking, "Who is this person who has someplace else to be? She must be in very high demand. And we'd better pay close attention, because this is our only opportunity. She's out of here, and off to her next audition."

Now, why does Albert Hague make that recommendation? It's not so you can cut in line or act like a diva. It's because it tells the auditors something about who you are. It says you're not a desperate hopeful who'll wait as long as they want. And it says you have other opportunities. And maybe more importantly, it nurtures your sense of dignity. I'm not telling you to do this. In fact, you probably shouldn't, since these days a thirty-minute wait is hardly unusual. I just want you to *imagine* it. Think about the idea that you *could* leave after thirty minutes and let that idea work its way into your sense of your own value.

Albert Hague also says there is only one answer to the question "Why do you need to leave?" That answer, true or not, is "I have another audition." "What's it for?" "I'm superstitious. I don't like to talk about it." That's also, by the way, the only reason you're ever late to an audition. No one wants to know that you hit traffic or got on the wrong train. That means you didn't plan well, and that means that you didn't have enough respect for the project to get yourself there on time, and that means that the same thing could happen if you booked the job. "Why were you late?" "I was held up at another audition." "What was it for?" "I'm superstitious. I don't like to talk about it." Hague's suggestions support the idea that the actor is worthy of respect.

In keeping with this idea of personal dignity, I encourage you to cultivate your own set of policies for yourself and your career. Know what is or is not acceptable to you, and what you will or won't do. An example of a policy is the question of whether or not you do nudity. If you don't do nudity, it doesn't matter what the job is, or who the director is, how much money or prestige is offered. You just don't do it, so there's nothing to discuss. Some people won't play certain kinds of roles, or smoke on camera, or use certain language. I have a policy: I don't allow people to abuse me. I would gladly lose any job rather than stand for that. If someone treats me in a way that is truly abusive, I calmly smile and say, very graciously, "I don't allow people to speak to me this way." And if the behavior continues, I wish the person well, and I leave. Not everyone needs to have that policy. I do, because I'm extremely sensitive and if I let myself be disrespected, it haunts me. So I can't afford it. But you may have other policies. Some actors have told me they reject roles that, they feel, present demeaning stereotypes. Others refuse to play characters who smoke, or use drugs. Regardless of what your policies are, it's good to have them. Personal policies contribute to your sense of power and individuality and your awareness of your own will, and make you feel less like you're at the mercy of others, less like you're destined to be blown about by whatever wind comes along. Knowing you have some firm limits and a sense of how you want to design your career can fortify your self-esteem.

And all of this internal work becomes part of what you bring into a room. You come in as a person of substance, authority, and professionalism—someone who has a say in what happens to you, not just another desperate, needy, "I'll-do-anything" actor in a sea of actors all vying for attention. You get to be your own island. Without saying anything, you exude effortless individuality simply by virtue of honoring your own dignity.

A Word about "Workshops"

Now, while we're on the subject (and still killing time in the waiting room), I'm going to wade into some controversial waters for a moment and tell you why I'm against those so-called casting director "workshops" that are often, in truth, no more than thinly veiled opportunities to make contacts. There has been much heated discussion on this issue and I don't expect this will be the final word. But I want to talk about it in terms of our topic: conducting your career with a sense of dignity.

When you pay for a meeting with a casting person, it says something about your status. It identifies you as someone who has to pay to be considered for acting work. It puts the other person high above you—so high that you have to give him or her money to look at you. And unfortunately, I don't think the people you're paying to meet have much respect for people willing to pay to meet them. Early in my career, I attended one of these things. A few moments in, the casting person I'd paid to meet recognized one of the actors in the room. "What are you doing here?" she asked, "You're a good actor."

Charging a fee for a job interview is generally considered unethical. Imagine if AT&T's Director of Human Resources taught "workshops" on how to get a job with AT&T and charged a fee to potential employees who were taking the workshop as a way of getting a foot in the door. That operation would be shut down fast. Or what if you were hoping to work as a waiter at that hoity-toity bistro Chez Pretentioso but in order to meet the restaurant manager, you had to pay to take his class about how to get hired there? What? Forget that. I'll go down the block to Chez Snooterie, thank you very much. Taking part in an unethical activity shows desperation, not dignity.

Now, to be clear (as clear as one can be when describing a somewhat muddy nuance), *some* casting director workshops are bona fide educational opportunities rather than job interviews. (Most often, these are ongoing classes rather than one-nighters, and most often, they're taught by people who've been at this a while and have learned something about how to help actors improve their skills.) Those are very different, and totally kosher. But *you* know the difference. Are you learning? Or are you auditioning and making contacts? You know your motives. It's fine to pay for education from a qualified instructor. In fact, I strongly encourage that. It's wrong to pay just to be in the presence of someone who can hire you.[7]

---

[7] For more on the legalities, see The Krekorian Talent Scam Prevention Act of 2009 and SAG-AFTRA's Rule 11.

The challenging thing is that these "workshops" can some-times be effective. Some even call them a "necessary evil" and say there's nothing we can do, claiming they're the only way to promote oneself. But throughout this book, we've been revisiting and questioning ideas that have become lodged in our thinking as accepted norms—givens. I encourage you to do that in this case as well. I invite you to take a fearless look at the big picture of your career and think about how you want to conduct yourself, and how you want to be perceived. Don't sacrifice your dignity for the sake of a possible contact.

If you disagree with me on this controversial topic (many do, and I'm well acquainted with the opposing arguments), I make no judgment. You have to be the boss of your own career. But if you do decide to participate, I encourage you to do so with dignity, to carry yourself proudly, as a mem-ber of a noble profession, and to reject treatment that puts you at a lower status than the person you're paying to meet. Remember what our friend Milton Katselas says: "You have got to win—you cannot lose if you come that way."

CHAPTER SEVEN

NERVES IN THE LAB

W ell, they've been calling in actors and now there are only a few ahead of you, so there couldn't be a better time to talk about the actor's N word—nervousness—since it seems to be the biggie for most of us.

If you find that nervousness is making it difficult for you to audition joyfully—or even comfortably—first understand that this is not an inevitable or permanent condition; it's a puzzle to be solved, nothing more. If you wake up with a weird throbbing in your pinky, you don't think, "Well, that's it. I have a throbbing pinky. That's just how it is." No. You start to solve the puzzle. "What's causing that? How do I fix it? Aha! I've been hitting my pinky with a mallet in my sleep." Strange, but OK. Solution: lock up all the mallets before bedtime. Think of your nervousness as something you can look at, analyze, work on, and at least reduce. And by the way, you don't need to get rid of nervousness entirely. Nerves can be exciting and energizing. We just don't want them to be debilitating. To quote English footballer Steve Bull, "Nerves and butterflies are fine—they're a physical sign that you're mentally ready and eager. You have to get the butterflies to fly in formation, that's the trick."

To that end, let's head into the lab and put our nervousness under a microscope. We're going to dissect it, pull it apart, take some x-rays, and see how far we can whittle it down.

First, let's be sure you're making an accurate diagnosis. As a young actor, I studied with a brilliant acting teacher, the late Doug Moston. Doug used to say that before you conclude you're nervous, you should check to make sure that what you're feeling is really nervousness. He said to ask yourself, "*Am* I nervous? Or am I just excited?" The two emotions feel almost identical, and have very similar physiological manifestations—increased heartbeat, the rush of adrenaline, et cetera. Sometimes, you'll find that what you're feeling isn't really nervousness at all, but just the natural excitement that often accompanies performing.

Many actors experience nerves as a knee-jerk reaction. They've unconsciously glued the idea of nervousness to the idea of auditioning, as if one automatically follows the other as sure as Tuesday follows Monday. They think, "Audition! I must be nervous!" without stopping to assess whether they really are. You know, you might not be. So don't make it an automatic assumption.

Strange as it may sound, many actors feel *obligated* to feel nervous about auditioning, as if it's what's supposed to happen, like it's the right way to do it. So what do they do? They fulfill that obligation by making themselves nervous.

And here's a little psychological theory of mine. I believe that some of us make ourselves nervous because we're subconsciously concerned that *not* being nervous might somehow suggest a lack of humility. How's *that* for twisted? We're saying, "Don't worry, I'm not arrogant or anything. See? I'm nervous." Well, now, is that helping? No. It's not helping you in any way. Confidence isn't arrogance, and nervousness isn't humility.

Others have told me they worry that if they're not nervous, they're not engaged, not focused, not on their game. That one also seems pretty warped when you see it in print, doesn't it? Not much logic there. In my experience, nervousness *hurts* your focus and concentration, rather than helping it.

All of this is to say, it's important to understand that it's one hundred percent OK to have an audition and *not* be nervous.

In fact, once you've embraced the knowledge that (say it with me, now) you're not getting the fucking job, it's very likely that you'll find you're no longer nervous at auditions. You may be able to relax and enjoy yourself. In fact, many who've taken my workshop have claimed just such results. Because if you already know you're not going to get the job, there are no stakes, nothing to worry about, no chance of "nailing it" or doing it perfectly, and thus, nothing to be nervous about, just an opportunity to enjoy the "chance to act on a Thursday."

But let's say that you really *are* nervous, rather than excited, and that you haven't made it up; it's a real feeling. Fair enough. Let's take a closer look.

You know what very few of us do when we're feeling nervous? Ask ourselves what we're nervous *about*. So, let's slow down and take a look at what we're dealing with. To do that, I want to first look at the deeper, more subconscious fears—your most irrational, primal, inner-child terrors, the ones that don't make any sense. For example, some actors, when they think about auditioning, feel like they're going to die, fall through the floor, or pass out. Some feel like they could go insane, or get yelled at, or ridiculed, or humiliated, or punished. Don't ask yourself to be rational just yet; we'll get to that. For now, see how far into the cave of the subconscious you can shine your flashlight, and see if you can figure out what that fear is for you. Because once you can name the crazy, irrational stuff, you can start getting rid of it.

My fear—I'll share with you, because we're close like that—is this: Way deep down inside me, I'm afraid that casting directors will think I'm such an awful actor that they'll yell at me, laugh at me, and order me to leave their office, offended that I ever dared to enter. I'm afraid they'll say, "You're a fake. You are no actor. And by calling yourself an actor, you're insulting all the real actors out there in the waiting room. You have no idea what you're doing. You don't belong in a professional show business office like this. Get out of here and never come back!"

If your fear is the same as mine, that's fine. I don't have it copyrighted. (Trust me, a lot of us share that one.) But figure out what your deepest, most irrational fears are. And then, as an exercise, ask yourself how likely it is that those things will happen. Scale of one to ten. Like, I assume we all know that in reality, it's not very likely that anyone will yell at us and kick us out of an audition. But when we're nervous, we may need to remind ourselves of that. This kind of deliberate reflection helps you sort of crack open your nervousness and see what it looks like on the inside, which makes it much easier to disarm. It's like diffusing the irrational fear that there's a monster in the closet by actually turning on the light and checking.

(Oh come on. You've done it.)

Next, here are a few really dumb things that actors get nervous about, that you can get rid of right away.

- Forgetting or stumbling over lines. Holey moley! We get so worked up about this one. Many actors have a *terrible* dread of not saying the lines correctly. We have blown this one up in our minds to be the great unpardonable sin. It is not. You have to understand that casting people are usually taking in your appearance, your voice, your approach to the role . . . things like that . . . as opposed to your memorization skills. If you blow a line, so be it. It happens. Dive back in. No casting person in his right mind has ever said, "Well, I liked her for the part, until she messed up one of the lines. We can't work with someone like that!" That's just silly. Look up Aaron Paul's audition for the series *Breaking Bad*. It's on the Internet somewhere. He stumbled over a line or two. Not only wasn't he banished, he went on to star in the series.

Oh, there's one thing he *didn't* do. He didn't bail on the scene, beat himself up, lose his character, or freak out. He just picked up where he left off. No big deal.

- The second dumb thing to be nervous about is what I call the Kicked Out of Show Business scenario. That one goes like this: Do badly at one audition, and you're all washed up as an actor. Say goodbye to ever having a career. Because as you know, of course, there's a monthly international meeting of all the casting directors where they don hooded robes and chant in a mysterious tongue while they light ceremonial candles. And then they open The Big Book of Who's a Bad Actor, and invite members to step forward and report any new additions. The casting people cackle with evil delight as they ridicule the poor untalented souls behind their backs, then they add their names, rendering them Kicked Out of Show Business. The word goes out to all the agents, writers, directors, and producers (through their underground network of minions), and that actor is never hired again, anywhere. You all know that, right?

See how silly it sounds? But a good number of you have concocted just such a fantasy scenario, allowing this completely nonexistent danger to contribute to your all-too-existent nerves. It's hard for actors to hear this, but in reality, folks just aren't thinking about you that much. Even if you stink, no one is warning others about your offensive lack of ability. They simply have more important things to do.

So can we throw that one out? Good.

- And then, there's just the general fear of sucking. (Anyone? Just me? Ahhhh, now I see some hands raised. OK. I had a feeling some of you might relate to this one.) Now fear of sucking is this: we think that we'll walk into an audition and all of our abilities will abandon us. And whatever work we did to prepare for the audition will simply vanish. And we'll just simply suck.

  OK. Here's my dumb little exercise to put your fear of sucking into perspective. Now, every actor has a range in the quality of his work, from his best performance to his worst performance. Sometimes we're in the zone and sometimes we're just not. And there are some roles we connect with better than others. Right? OK. Let's chart that. There's no science here, so don't get too bogged down over accuracy. Hold out your right hand at a level that represents you on your best day, doing your best acting. Now, hold out your left hand at a level that's you on your worst day, doing your worst acting. Great. Take a look at where your hands are and commit to these levels, for the time being; let's say this is your quality range. Now, fear of sucking is the belief that you're going to be worse than where you currently have your left hand. Let me point out— that's impossible. Because you just showed me you on your worst day. Look at your left hand. There it is. The worst you can ever be. Short of getting conked on the head and developing amnesia, you cannot be worse than your worst. You cannot simply lose all of your talent and technique as if you never had it. We have this mythology that says our abilities are tenuous, ever in danger of slipping away from us without warning. This is crazy. Looking at it in this visual, pseudoscientific way can help calm your nerves by dispensing with this truly dumb fear, that your capacity for suckage is a bottomless pit.

So what's left to be nervous about? Plenty. Some of the things we get nervous about are perfectly plausible. What if the casting person doesn't like your work? What if they don't think you're good? These things could absolutely happen. So now it's time for a game I call "And Then What?" Let's play.

What if the casting director thinks you're simply not a good actor? Could happen, right? OK. And then what? Well, she might not ever call you in for another audition. OK. And then what? Is your career ruined? Do you cease to be an actor? Or do you press on, audition for casting people who *do* like your work, and find a way to keep pursuing your calling? Hmmm . . . looks like the worst-case scenario isn't so awful.

What else is making you nervous? Here's one. What if you have a string of auditions that don't go well for you and your agent decides to drop you as a client? A lot of actors live in terror of that possibility. OK. Let's face it head on. What do you do if that happens? Quit? Die? Or find a way to continue your career? Do you think for one moment that I've never been dropped by an agent? Let me relieve you of that delusion; I've been dropped by *several* agents. And you know what? I lived to tell the tale.

It's really unfair to yourself to load up your audition with fears of what could happen if it doesn't go well. How are you supposed to perform a role for a few minutes when you're burdened with these hypotheticals? Dismantle them now by thinking through the very worst thing that could happen and asking yourself, "And then what?"

Now, at last, we're down to the part of nervousness that makes sense: the perfectly understandable discomfort of presenting oneself for evaluation and scrutiny, the fear of being embarrassed, or doing something wrong. You're going to be performing in front of people, and you want to be evaluated positively, and many of us are insecure by nature, so, it makes total sense that you'd be nervous. And honestly, no one can fault you for that.

But now we come to the "tough love" portion of this book—a truth that very few people will tell you. Here it is, friends: no one wants to deal with a nervous actor. No one. As understandable as nervousness is, if you *share* your nervousness, you're unlikely to get a positive response. Because—and I'm repeating it because I really want you to get it—*no one* wants to deal with a nervous actor.

In fact, if you think about it, no one wants to deal with a nervous member of *any* profession. Would you go to a nervous auto mechanic, a nervous accountant, a nervous headshot photographer? No. If your local grocery store had a nervous cashier, wouldn't you go out of your way to avoid her line? Parents, imagine you're interviewing babysitters. Given a choice, would you ever in a million years hire a babysitter who was nervous? Never! You certainly wouldn't want a nervous cab driver, hairstylist, or surgeon. But really, I don't even want to *ride an elevator* with a nervous person. I just don't want to be around that energy. Do you?

No, of course you don't. No one does. So, like it or not, you're not allowed to show nervousness at your auditions. Now that doesn't mean you're not allowed to *feel* nervous. It does mean that you're not allowed to *show* it. It is inappropriate to share that with casting people, because your nerves are not their problem. Their problem is getting their projects cast, and the last thing they want is to have to calm you down so you can audition, or worse, take a risk on someone who might have a meltdown backstage or on the set. This ain't therapy. You're nervous? Keep it to yourself. Otherwise, you're forcing *others* to experience it *with* you.

I think it's because actors deal with emotions, and our training teaches us to connect honestly with our unedited feelings, that we sometimes forget how to disguise those feelings in real life. In acting class, we openly reveal how things affect us. In business dealings, a professional veneer is often called for.

I had a great lesson in this while on tour with *The Producers*. I was in the ensemble, and I loved my job. I played twelve roles a night—all these crazy characters—and I was singing and dancing in a great big touring Broadway show for the first time in my life. I also happened to be understudying the enormous leading role of Max Bialystock, originated by Nathan Lane. So we're out on the road, playing Cleveland, and it's Sunday morning and the phone rings in my hotel room. It's the stage manager. He says, "Michael, our lead is out sick. You're playing Max Bialystock." Well . . . fuck. This sounds very glamorous and exciting so long as it's not happening to you. But all my blood drained to my feet and all I could think was, "That's impossible!" But then it occurred to me: I was in a situation in which I did not have the luxury of being nervous—at least not visibly so. Audience members were paying top ticket prices to see *The Producers* and dammit, they needed a Max Bialystock, not a nervous actor. On top of that, since we'd never had an understudy in the lead, my castmates were looking to me to see if we still had a show. I had to be the daddy. For their sakes, I could not show my nerves. It was sort of non-negotiable. As I walked through the stage door one of the dancers said, "Oh my God. I just heard. Are you nervous?" I gave her a confident smile and replied, "Nervous? Hell no, sweetheart. Let's get out there and kill it. See you on stage." Now, mind you, as soon as I was alone in the dressing room I whimpered like a small child. But no one except me—*no one*—knew I was nervous.

Now, I'm not going to leave you hanging with "Don't show anyone that you're nervous," and toddle off to write my next book. I still have a few more techniques for you to try that might help you manage those nerves.

But the reason I stress this idea of a taboo so vigorously is that there is some power in understanding that a behavior simply isn't allowed. Preachers and politicians aren't allowed to display nerves; that would make their listeners feel uneasy about their messages. Neither are schoolteachers, or lawyers, or tour guides. Every airline pilot has a first flight. He might be nervous. Is he allowed to display those nerves in front of his passengers? Absolutely not. Put yourself in that same category—not allowed—and you may find that's enough to enable you to keep your nerves well-hidden.

But even better? Work on being less nervous. In addition to the stuff we talked about at the beginning of this chapter and some of my suggestions from our chapter about the waiting room, there are two physical ways I know of to lessen nerves:

- Breathe. I know you think you're breathing. But I mean really breathe, deep and long, like they teach you in yoga class . . . I think. (What do I know? I've never been to a yoga class in my life.) Slowly, in through the nose and slowly out through the mouth. This works. I'm serious. I read somewhere[8] that this kind of deep, slow breathing does several great things at once. It calms you down and, at the

---

[8] Don't you love my ironclad, irrefutable resources?

same time, gives you energy; it releases endorphins, which make you happy; it gives you better mental clarity. It's like some kind of wonder drug, this breathing stuff. But you have to make yourself do it. It always seems like a dumb waste of time when you're wound up and intense about something. But I think it might just possibly be a lot dumber to know that this type of deep breathing helps and not make use of that knowledge. It's like placing two Advil tablets on the kitchen counter and wondering why you still have a headache. The medicine works so much better if you actually take it. *Make* yourself do it. I swear it works.

- Smile. They say that smiling, whether you're happy or not, sends a message to your brain that says you are. And it makes you happy. But really, is there any reason not to be? This stuff is supposed to be fun. We're not airlifting flood victims here; we're putting on a hat and singing a song. We're playing make-pretend. You want to have a laugh? Go into the rest room, look at yourself in the mirror, and think about the silliness of the task in which you're engaged. We get way too intense about what are, in truth, fairly goofy endeavors. You have every reason to smile.

As I mentioned earlier, many of the actors who've taken my workshop report that their index cards have been their best weapon against nerves. Load yours up with ideas that calm you down and remind you of the things you love about auditioning and, when you're feeling nervous, give those ideas some real thought.

And finally, remember your mantra. You're not getting the fucking job. What is there to be nervous about? You're worried they won't cast you? There's no mystery there. They won't. I think you'll find this reminder to be a pretty reliable nerve eliminator.

But what if none of the anti-nervous techniques you know is working and you just can't seem to calm yourself down? Or, what if something big is happening in your life and the result is that you're feeling some other powerful emotion you absolutely cannot shake—anger, grief, exhaustion? What if you just got dumped by your boyfriend or girlfriend? Or lost a friend or relative or a pet? Or had a car accident? And what if those emotions are overriding everything? What now?

Well, how about I give you a "safety net" to use just under those circumstances in which you can't seem to pull yourself together? (This is one of my favorite techniques.) If you're too nervous, angry, upset, sick, shaken, or exhausted to perform the way you'd like to, then the only alternative is to see if you can use what you're feeling. (As you'll see, this doesn't just work for auditions. It also works for performances. It's a technique to apply any time your mental state is overwhelming your ability to do your work.)

Years ago, I had an audition for a television show called *ER*. The role was a self-important community theatre director. Two of his performers have gotten into an on-stage fight that landed them both in the hospital emergency room. The agitated director is trying to hurry along the hospital staff in the hopes of salvaging the second act of his play.

I arrived at the audition to find the hallways packed with actors—all talented, working character guys, any of whom could have played the part. I couldn't imagine why they needed to see so many of us. And apparently, the casting session was running late because the producer was delayed. So we were all kept waiting for a very long time. At an hour and a half, I began to get frustrated. At two hours, I was getting edgy, and I fantasized about leaving. By the time I'd been there for two and a half hours, I was pissed off. So pissed off, in fact, that I just couldn't focus on anything but how mad I was. I couldn't let it go. And I thought, "This sucks! I was ready to audition when I got here, on time. And now my audition is fucked because I'm so pissed off I can't do what I'd planned on doing."

And that was when I realized: "Wait a minute! These emotions could be exactly what this character is experiencing." What a gift! So when they finally called my name, I decided to go in there and express exactly how mad I was, but to use the scene to do it. I didn't fight it. I used it. I saw their faces. They were stunned by how real my frustration seemed. That's because it *was* real. They'd done me a big favor by making me wait. I was *fuming*. And that time, believe it or not, I actually *did* get the fucking job.

I was once doing a production of *Ragtime*, playing a poor, struggling immigrant with a little daughter. Sophia, my "show child," was a dry, witty, sarcastic ten-year-old, and we were crazy about each other. Thinking I was teaching her something about theatre (as the older, wiser, more experienced mentor), I once explained, "Now, Sophia, I just want to warn you: there are parts of this show where I may yell or scream or cry. That's all part of the acting. I just don't want you to be scared." And the little smartass looked up at me and responded dryly, "Well, wouldn't my character *be* scared?" Ooh, the ungrateful wretch. She was 100% right. She was going to *use* the fear and make the scene even more real. And so it turned out, she taught *me* something.

I recently coached a brilliant actress friend for an audition. I arrived at her apartment to find her aggravated and unsettled. "What's going on?" I asked. "My stupid, suck-ass agents just got me the script for this fucking film *yesterday*. The assholes had it Friday. I could have studied it over the fucking weekend, but *no!* So now I don't know what I'm doing, and now I have no time to prepare this shit, and so, you know, I'm kinda pissed." "OK," I said. "So, let's dive in. What's the role?" "Oh, she's this bitter chick. It says she could teach sailors to curse, and she's stuck in this job she hates, and—" And I said, "Uh-huh." And she said, "I know. I know." (We'd worked together before.) I told her to stop trying to get over being angry. I suggested she tell the casting directors the whole story about her stupid agents, but use the dialogue and the scene to do it. She could be absolutely truthful without them ever knowing what was going on. Guess who got a callback?

OK. Forgive me. I have to drop a huge name in order to relate this story. I recently played (I still can't believe I'm about to type this) Robert De Niro's brother. Fucking De Niro. Me, with my minimal training, acting with one of the greats of our time. Now look, I'm talking to fellow actors here, so I think you'll understand this. When I got to the set for the first day of filming, I did *NOT* think, "Say! I'm working with Robert De Niro. I must be quite a fine actor." Oh, no, my friends, just the opposite. I shrunk up into a dark, ugly little ball of insecurity inside. No one knew. But I kept thinking, "Oh, God. Those are the *real* actors. I don't belong here. They're going to know I'm a fake. I'm going to look awful next to them." And I got very quiet, and felt very small. It was pretty intense, and I couldn't pull myself out of it. I was shy. I didn't introduce myself to anyone. But what saved me was that I've been teaching this stuff for a while, and, even though I felt miserable, I took comfort in the fact that the character I was playing was a quiet sort who lived in his brother's shadow and looked up to him. And so that became my performance. It was the only choice I could make that day.

These examples, however, all cite cases in which the actor's real emotions were at least somewhat apropos. But what if what you're feeling doesn't "match"? What if your powerful, unshakeable emotions aren't the "right" ones? Good news: often, you can *still* use what you're feeling. The people watching don't know your specifics; all they'll see is that something real is happening inside of you. Emotions can pass as other emotions. The intensity of nervousness, for example, can look like anger, terror, excitement, lust, insanity, ambition, shock, greed, rage, confusion, and so on. Play the truth, and the viewer will often make the leap. ("Look how her hands are shaking. She must really love him.")

And here's what's even cooler. Using what you're really, truly feeling (instead of forcing what you're supposed to feel but can't) can lead to fascinating, compelling, unusual choices. Who says the nun always has to be serene, or that the drug addict has to be shaky, or that the bully has to be loud? (Think of Meryl Streep's brilliant choice in *The Devil Wears Prada*; she played a tyrant who never raised her voice. Or Tom Noonan's offbeat and enigmatic Detective Huntley on *Damages*; his friendly, seemingly trusting interrogations kept his suspects guessing what he was really thinking. Neither was an obvious choice.) If you can't shake an emotion you're feeling—I mean, really just can't shake it—then dare to use it. You aren't getting the fucking job anyway. Might as well try my favorite technique as an experiment.

Let's explore . . .

The Numbers Exercise

This is an exercise for learning to apply your real emotions to a scene. (It was a favorite of the aforementioned Doug Moston, from whom I learned it.) Now, this one is challenging, but can produce spectacular results. It helps you get off what you think you're *supposed* to be feeling in a scene and work with your true emotional state. This exercise works best in a group setting, like a class. But I include it here because I think it clarifies the overall concept.

1) Start by talking about how you're feeling. Be completely honest. Allow yourself to experience

and express your emotional state, describing what you're thinking and feeling and where you feel it in your body. Take a physical inventory. Note everything that's going on. If it changes, stay connected and continue to convey what you're experiencing from moment to moment. Try not to diffuse the feelings with jokes. Just feel them.

2) Now, as you continue expressing all those things, let go of the words, and replace them with numbers. It doesn't matter which numbers, or the order in which you use them. The numbers are just to get you used to expressing yourself with something other than your own words. Think of the numbers as a nonsense language, and use them to continue to talk about your true, honest feelings.

3) Next, begin your dialogue,[9] but *do not act*. Just continue expressing your true, honest, unmanipulated feelings, using the script instead of your own words. Don't worry about making emotional sense; just move forward on faith. This isn't easy. It's always tempting to start crafting a performance once you begin to understand what

---

[9] In my workshops, I use a series of short, generic speeches I've written especially for this exercise. Once the actors have talked about the emotions they're feeling, then moved to numbers for a bit, I hand them these pages at random. They never know what kind of monologue they'll be reading, which makes it easier to resist applying anything calculated to the words. I've included these speeches in the back of this book for your use.

the lines are about. But for this exercise, it's important not to do that. If you catch yourself starting to play the words, go back to numbers and reconnect with your true feelings. Then, when you're ready to once again communicate your current state of mind, use the words on the page.

I love this exercise. What you'll often find is that classmates will tell you it was some of the most honest, compelling acting they've ever seen you do. Sometimes, the choice isn't at all right for the scene. Even in those instances, it's engaging to watch an actor telling the truth about his true feelings while using someone else's words.

This idea of using your true mental state in presenting your audition scene, however, is all Plan B. Plan A is to have success using the techniques I listed earlier to get yourself calm, focused, and able to do your work. But if you *can't*, then making use of the emotions you're unable to put aside is one way to avoid inflicting those emotions on your auditors. Mastering this method also knocks out the anxiety that comes from thinking your nervousness (or anger, or grief, or whatever) is going to sink your ability to perform. Now you have a safety net.

And what if the worst-case scenario happens? What if your nervousness is so bad that nothing makes it any better—not even the suggestions in this book? And what if that happens consistently? One, consider quitting the profession. I'm not joking. Life is too short for constant agony. As the traditional wisdom dictates, if you can be happy in any other profession, do it. Or, two, if the idea of quitting is repulsive to you, then you'll have to find a way to deal with the nerves. This is a profession that (for all but a few actors) requires auditioning. So if you can't quit the business, and can't conquer your nerves, consider working with a specialist. Try hypnotherapy, psychotherapy, acupuncture, life coaching. Or try putting in a prayer request at church, or feng shui. Just understand that you have to do something. Bringing your nervousness into auditions will diminish your already nearly nonexistent chances of ever getting hired and, more to my point, make it difficult to enjoy your life as an actor.

And on that discouraging note . . .

CHAPTER EIGHT

DOORWAY TO THE UNKNOWN

A h. It's finally time to go into our audition. The person before us has just come out and they'll be calling our name in a matter of seconds. So let's talk about what happens next.

Have you ever seen that show *Curb Appeal*? It's one of those home improvement shows on HGTV (Home & Garden Television). On *Curb Appeal,* people who are trying to sell their houses meet design experts who help them improve their chances by sprucing up the view from the curb—the houses' front exteriors. I learned an interesting thing on *Curb Appeal* that has been confirmed for me by several real estate people. They say that the biggest part of the decision to buy a home happens in the seven seconds it takes a potential buyer to get from his car door to the front door of the house. If he likes the outside, he's inclined to like the inside. If he dislikes the outside, it's unlikely the inside will do anything to change his initial opinion. (This is an example of a theory called "confirmation bias," the idea that there's a human tendency to accept evidence that conforms to our existing beliefs and reject evidence that contradicts those beliefs.)

Now, what does that have to do with us? Well, the same is true of auditioning. Casting folks start making decisions about you from the moment you're through the door. So how you enter a room—your "curb appeal"—is vitally important. Now, I don't want that to make you tense. It just means that we have to be conscious about what we convey when we enter a room.

I have a theory that within seconds, people decide whether they're in the presence of an amateur or a professional, whether you've brought something to them or are asking for something from them.

If you've ever gone to see little kids do a play at school or camp (and if you haven't, put down this book right away and do it, because you'll never see anything funnier or cuter), you might have witnessed a great example of what I'm talking about. There's this thing that sometimes happens that always makes me smile. Everyone's sitting in the audience, waiting for the show. The lights go down. We all get quiet. And then, instead of the show starting, there's this . . . pause . . . and after a few too many seconds, there's this funny moment when everyone realizes that something is off, because nothing is happening; you're all just sitting there in the dark. Right? Have you been there? The audience starts to giggle as they realize that the kids don't know to start the show. It's usually at this point that the drama teacher sheepishly tiptoes backstage. And a few moments later, you hear little feet scurrying around behind the curtain in a panic as little voices whisper loudly, "It started! Go!" "Get ready, you guys, I'm serious!"

And then the curtain goes up. And you clap extra hard to encourage the little tykes and assure them that there's nothing to be embarrassed about. At that point, you, the audience members, are taking care of them, the performers. And that's perfectly fine. Because they're little kids and you want to encourage them. But if you had to do that for the performers on Broadway after paying $6,500 a ticket (or whatever it is these days), you'd be far less charmed by the whole situation. You don't want to help them. You want them to just do the show while you relax and enjoy it. Right?

When I teach, I try to project several things right from the beginning of the class: that I'm glad to be there, that I'm comfortable, that I'm happy to see everyone, that we're going to have a good time, that there's nothing to worry about, nothing to be intimidated by, and that I'm here to help those who've come to the workshop.

But for the sake of my point, let me now open up my brain for you so you can take a look at the strange world inside. I'm just as neurotically insecure as any other actor you know. (Did you think I was immune?) And so, often I'm thinking, "Who the hell am I to be teaching? These people are going to be bored to death. They're going to feel like they wasted their time and their money. I don't think they like me. They're looking at me like I'm full of shit." . . . and so on. This is even worse when I look out and see colleagues—people who work as much as (or even more than) I do. Or really pretty girls—they can make me nervous too. And sometimes I've just had a discouraging day and I feel like a loser. Now, here's my point. I don't share *any* of that with the people in my classes. Why? Because it would be unfair to them, and inappropriate. That's not why we're here. They came for me to help them, not to deal with my insecurities.

Right?

OK . . . so here it is . . . the big one. The reason you bought this book. This is The Michael Kostroff Golden Rule of Auditioning:

Take care of them. Never ask them to take care of you.

I'll repeat that. Take care of them. Never ask them to take care of you. You are the doctor; they're the patients. You're the expert; they're the people in need of expertise. They're needy. They need to find the right actor. You're there to see if you can help. Offer something. Ask for nothing.

Now listen to me. If you do this *one thing*, you will be doing the 180° opposite of what most actors do at auditions. Do this *one thing*—take care of them, don't ask them to take care of you—and you will see casting people relax and warm up to you like you wouldn't believe. Most actors have the wrong idea. They go to an audition hoping to have an experience that makes them feel good about themselves as actors. They want compliments and encouragement. They want to leave and be able to say, "I think she liked me. I think I did OK. I felt good about it. Maybe she'll like me enough to bring me back." They want to feel that they're worthy and belong in this profession and that their careers are moving forward. That's what most actors hope to get out of an audition. And they unconsciously place that burden on the person who's casting. But really, that's not what casting sessions are about. Casting sessions are *not* scheduled so that actors can have opportunities to feel good about themselves. That's why *therapy* sessions are scheduled. As it happens, *casting* sessions are scheduled in the hopes of solving casting problems. That's the purpose of those meetings. And you're there because you might be able to assist them.

If this were a scene in a play or movie, the main character would be the casting director, not you. We'd be watching the casting director try to fill a role as these wacky actors came in and out. That's what the scene would be about. The audience would be tracking the casting director's journey, and rooting for him to succeed.

When I go in for an audition, I try to project the following message (without saying it out loud, of course): "I understand you need an actor. Maybe I can help." As an auditioner, you mustn't ask for anything or need anything from the people watching you present your work. You're there only to give—to present yourself as one of the choices—one item on the menu of actors which they're free to choose or not, without worrying about you, your feelings, your needs, your career, your finances, your hopes, your dreams, or your self-esteem. Reflect on that for a minute. It's a very different approach, isn't it?

Let's put it another way. In the civilian world, when a company is embarking on a new endeavor, they'll often call in a consultant—one with expertise in that particular area—to advise them. These people are brought in to show the staff how to do something they don't know how to do. It may be some new process, a new marketing direction, updating systems, increasing efficiency, or any number of other things.

That's you: the acting consultant. A writer writes a script. A producer agrees to produce the piece. The producer hires a director and a production team. And then they say, "Uh-oh. Look at all these words. What's the deal with that? What do we do with them?" "I know! Let's call in some actors. *They'll* know what to do!" And they put out the call. And here you come—the proverbial knight (or knight . . . ess) on a white horse—and show them one possible way that the role could be presented! Imagine their relief!

Sometimes the help you provide is showing them what they *don't* want. That, too, is a valuable service, as it may help them further define their needs. And that's what you're there for, to help them figure things out. A consultant isn't looking for a job. A consultant is there to assist with someone *else's* job.

By the way, this doesn't only apply when you're specifically invited to audition by name and given an appointment time. Whenever a casting call is put out, actors are being invited to come in as consultants. If you fit the character description, you have an opportunity to help by presenting your unique take on that part.

It's like being a carpet salesman. Come in with your samples. Show the buyer some options. They want stain-resistant? You have that. Comes in seven colors. They want low-pile? Shag? You have that too. Show your samples, answer any questions, leave your card, and move on with your day.

Whether you're a beginner or a seasoned pro, now is the time to start thinking of yourself as someone who can help—someone who, if people are looking for an actor, might be able to provide the answers to their casting prayers. One of my Audition Psych 101 alumni was told by a director, "Thank God you walked through the doors of that audition room." When you're there to help, and to take care of them, you can be the one who makes the auditors breathe a sigh of relief, confident that they're at last in the presence of a professional who is doing nothing more than offering his services.

I have an exercise I do in my class. It's called "Through the Door," and it works like this: I have a group of actors leave the room, then reenter one by one. Each person is to come in and, in some way, convey that he's going to take care of us, and we don't have to worry about him. He can talk or not talk. He can make us laugh, make us take notice, stand there quietly, even intimidate us, but he must not ask us to take care of him in any way. He has to let us know that the situation is being handled and we can relax. Each person takes his own cue to enter, and sits down when he feels done. If the remaining members of the class feel an actor has asked to be taken care of, they send him back to try again.

It's interesting for the participants to see how quickly this willingness and ability to take care of us is either conveyed or not conveyed, and how many different ways there are of conveying it. I've seen people come in sweet, sexy, deadpan, dangerous, gentle, flamboyant, elegant, and even shy, and still succeed at making us feel taken care of.

One thing I discourage actors from doing is making cutesy entrances or exits, or using gimmicks or catch phrases. I'm shuddering just thinking about it. These are the things actors think will make them memorable or charming or appealing, but generally just make them annoying. A casting director friend told me about an actor who'd say, before walking out of her office, "See ya on the set!" What is this? Power of suggestion? "Look how confident I am!"? It does nothing to convince anyone to cast you. It's just cutesy. "See ya on the set" (wink). All my friend could think was, "No, you won't." Gimmicks come across as substitutes for substance. They make the auditors think you probably don't have anything usable to bring to the table so you're trying to distract them by juggling colorful scarves and telling jokes. It's like those contestants on TV singing competitions who wear weird clothes or bring in props. You know they're not going to be good singers.

There is this idea we have as actors that we have to *do* something or *become* something or *sell* something in order to convince the casting person to consider us once we're in the room. Not necessarily true.

Each of us has an essence about us that we tend take for granted, because it's just part of our DNA. We don't have to work to show it; we don't have to sell it. It's just there, and people experience it, even if we're unaware of it. That essence is working for us as soon as we walk through the door.

This idea of having an essence is all a bit mysterious. For some reason, certain actors seem instantly castable as construction workers, or femme fatales, or professors, or troublemakers, or overachievers. Some people look like they play the violin, or know about politics, or work as a stripper, or own memorabilia. Some people look trustworthy. Some look conniving. Who the hell knows why? But if you look at a stranger and ask yourself, "Would he return my lawnmower if I loaned it to him?" chances are you'll have an opinion. And because of this mysterious thing I'm calling "essence," sometimes, walking through the door, you're already in the "yes" column; you're already enough.

Now, if you've been given an appointment to audition, that means someone already thinks you look like the right type. But even if you haven't, it's not as if you enter at zero, as a blank, and have to start from scratch to demonstrate that you're right for a part. All the things that make you unique are already working. Maybe you don't have to try so hard.

Now, while we're on this, I'll make another point. It's very valuable to get to know how people see you. Because for some roles, you may want to tailor that first impression a bit. You can really help the casting folks out by suggesting the character with your manner. Now, don't come into the room *in* character. That really freaks people out. Rather, be the version of yourself that best suits the role. I'll explain. I play a lot of lawyers. And when I go in for those lawyer roles, I help the casting directors by wearing a suit and by being my most composed, professional self. I show my serious side, not my goofball side, because if they're casting a serious lawyer, showing my goofball side makes their job harder, and I'm there to help. If I'm auditioning for the role of a flamingly effeminate best friend, I'll be a little more fluid, let the quips and sarcasm fly, but still be me, more or less. So that they're already thinking, "Yes . . . I'm comfortable with him in this part."

I have a colleague of whom I'm very fond. He's a big hulk of a man, with huge muscles, long, wild hair, and a beard. His stock-in-trade is playing big, dangerous macho types—Russian wrestlers, backwoods gas station attendants, good-ol'-boy womanizers, and sweaty, threatening thugs. In real life, he couldn't be more different from the characters he plays. In real life, he's an incredibly warm, kind-hearted, gay, spiritual, supportive angel of a man who has a loving smile for everyone he meets. Now, this guy is *really* good at his work. In character, he's more macho than I could ever hope to be. The man oozes beer, testosterone, and danger. But I had to counsel him to hide his lovely, soft nature when first meeting casting people because he was confusing them. They had a hard time trusting this actor's marvelous ability to jump into these crazy, hyper-masculine characters. He needed, strange as it might sound, to *help* the casting folks by being a little less friendly and a little less accessible—not a jerk, mind you, just less of a lovable teddy bear. So think about the character you're auditioning to play, and give the casting people a nice, helpful "warm-up" in how you relate to them before doing the scene, *without acting.*

And finally, enter with the authority of a professional. Even if you're not a professional, you need to adopt that status for the duration of your audition, because it helps you come across as a more confident, pleasant person to be around, and helps the people on the other side of the table relax.

CHAPTER NINE

THOSE MYSTERIOUS CREATURES WHO CAST

Well, we're finally in the room. Amazed that it took us this long? That just tells you how many of these sneaky potential psychological pitfalls there are before we even get here, and how many ways we actors can create completely unnecessary anxieties about doing what we love.

Crossing that threshold into the casting office (or rehearsal studio or onto the stage) has now brought us face to face with that mysterious individual on the other side of the table—the one who'll be watching our performance today. (For the purposes of discussion, we'll call this creature a casting director, but it may sometimes be a writer, a director, a producer, a musical director, a choreographer, a dance captain, or a stage manager.) These are the people who—we've now decided—we're going to take care of, rather than asking them to take care of us. So let's get to know them a bit, and re-examine the way we interact with them.

Many, many actors have a skewed image of casting people. They see them as these terrifying, intimidating gods, sitting high up on a mountain, their fierce thunderbolts aimed at our little heads, and we must place our gifts daintily at the foot of the mountain and slowly back away while bowing, hoping they'll have pity and not smite us.

Well, that view doesn't really work for our purposes. It definitely doesn't make for your best auditioning. And plus, it's kind of weird. These are, after all, simply people, trying to do a job, just like us. Really. We're all of us just trying to do our work and do it well.

Now, some actors, in attempting to steel themselves against the sting of rejection and regain a sense of power, go to the other extreme. These bitter and misguided souls have developed such disdain for casting folks that it oozes from every pore the moment they enter the room. "Who are these gate-keepers," they'll bitch to their friends, "and what gives them the right to evaluate my art?" Guess what? That frame of mind's not helping either. People can tell when you have a chip on your shoulder—even if you think you're hiding it— and it makes them disinclined to work with you. It's also hard to act with all that inner indignation. If you're bitter, work it out on your own, and leave it outside. It is not your ally.

So here's the new equation. Give casting people, producers, and directors their status . . . but not at the expense of yours.

They're professionals, and so are you. They make art, and so do you. You're having a meeting. Maybe they'll decide to collaborate. That's all. Their project needs actors. So you belong in that room just as much as they do. Yes, true, they're the people who will be making the decisions about whether you move on, but that doesn't lessen your status; that's just casting people doing the job they were hired to do. You do yours, let them do theirs, and resist the inclination to think of either of you as anything but equals.

To that end, it might be helpful to learn a bit more about them.

So . . . who *are* these people, and what do they expect from us? Well, contrary to popular actor mythology, casting people aren't a tribe with common characteristics. They don't have those secret meetings we've imagined. They don't all know each other. Turns out, each one is a full-fledged individual. I know one casting director who danced on Broadway, one who believes in aliens, one who's dating a transsexual, one who used to do stand-up, one who plays in a band on the weekends, one who's always looking for a boyfriend, one with an adopted daughter, and several who've had to overcome major personal adversity. Some of them truly love actors, and many think of us as pals and equals. And yes, there are some who look down their noses at us and treat us with condescension. But the point is, it's time you stopped thinking of casting people as if they're all part of one big, multiheaded monster. At the end of the day, casting people are individuals, just like you and me, with quirks and assets and shortcomings. That's why asking what casting directors look for in an audition is like asking what dentists order at restaurants. For each one, the answer is unique. I know that sounds like it should be obvious, but the weird behavior of a lot of actors tells me it's far from it.

Shocking Truths about Casting People
Here are some things you may not know about the good people on the other side of the desk.

- Most of them are freelancers. When each job ends, they have to look for the next one. Sometimes that causes concern. (Sound familiar at all?)

- They have bosses—the people who hired them—for whom they're anxious to do a good job so they can get hired again.

- Until the last role is cast on a particular project, they sweat a bit. What if they don't find the right actor, at the right price, who meets with the approval of all who get a say in casting? Sometimes, they have to try to accommodate four producers with seven opinions. It can be stressful.

- Here's something else you may not know. Casting people want to like you. They're not hoping for the chance to reject someone. (I'm sure there are some sadistic sons of bitches who do relish making actors feel bad, but they're few and far between.) Casting directors want you to be right for the role because if you're right for the role, they can sleep that night, knowing they have at least one good choice. Why *wouldn't* they root for you? You're the one who can save their asses and make them look good in front of their bosses. You never thought of it that way, did you? The casting person wants to be able to say, in essence, "Look what I found!" and open the door, revealing you.

- As I mentioned previously, they also don't always know what they want. Sometimes there are disagreements among members of creative teams about what a character should be. Other times they're just blank slates, open to seeing what the actors bring in. Often their ideas about a character morph during the process. You might even be the one to show them what they want. It happens all the time.

- Some casting directors have a good understanding of how actors do their work—indeed, some are former actors themselves. But some don't have a clue. For these folks, good acting is like fire to the caveman. They know it has value ("Ogk. Fire good. Fire man's friend."), but they don't know where it comes from, exactly, or what makes it happen ("Ogk. Not know where fire come from."). Certainly they know when they see a performance they like, but they don't necessarily know how you got there. They need you to help them by showing it to them, and not confusing them with the details of the process.

The Legend of the Evil Casting Director
Actors talk a lot about rude or abusive casting people, as if we encounter them on a regular basis. I believe that's a

vastly inflated fiction of ours. Most of the casting people I've met—in fact, I'd say the overwhelming majority—are perfectly friendly and nice. If you're having a different experience, it might be because you've been burdening them with your personal needs. Think about it; it makes sense. If you were a casting person, trying to find actors for a project, you might justifiably resent being asked to take care of a nervous, neurotic, insecure actor. That isn't the job they signed on for. And that might be what sometimes makes them surly. To a less experienced auditioner, these casting people might seem like assholes. But actors may not realize the extent to which they're triggering the less-than-welcoming behavior.

Let's dwell on that last point for just a moment. As I said earlier, most casting people want to like you. They truly do. But that doesn't mean they want to save you, reassure you, take care of you, or act as your parent or therapist. And I also think that when you project that kind of neediness or desperation, people respond accordingly. They might not even know why they're being less than pleasant, but my guess is that by presenting yourself as someone of a lower status, with lower value, you've basically invited them to mistreat you. Your behavior has informed them that you're unworthy of their respect.

I hear people sometimes give the advice, "Just believe in yourself and be confident." I think that advice is bullshit, and completely impractical. If you don't believe in yourself, you can't just start, nor can you just decide to be confident. But what you can do is hone your ideas of what is and isn't appropriate, and what is and isn't effective. And you can keep those insecurities to yourself, like a true professional.

Coming in like you're an infiltrator who snuck into the casting office and whose worth is lower than the carpet will cue casting people to treat you as such. But come in like a pro and 98% of the time, you'll be treated in a perfectly respectful way.

And even if you do encounter the mythical beast known as the Evil Casting Director, remember: they still need to cast the role. I've heard actors complain, "Well, I *would* have had a shot if the casting director hadn't been such a jerk." Not so. Remember, everyone who goes in is meeting the same jerk, so it's a level playing field. And that jerk *still* has to cast someone. Maybe the poor fool never learned that bullying doesn't bring out the best in people. Pity him; it's going to take him a lot longer to find a cast.

Bullies, by the way, often back down when confronted. You might as well try it. Nothing to lose. You're not getting the fucking job anyway. Why allow someone to demean you on top of it? Many years ago, an LA actress friend of mine was auditioning for the role of Fantine in *Les Misérables*, a woman of strength who is mistreated but retains her dignity. She had the misfortune to be auditioning for a notoriously nasty casting person who stopped her mid-song and said, "Stop! Stop! I don't know why we even bother holding auditions in LA None of you people are any good, and you definitely can't sing. And besides, you're not a Fantine. I don't even think you're an actress—" It was at this point that my brave friend said calmly, "You know, I'm going to stop you. I don't really care if you like my singing or not. I'm a very good singer, and I've been paid a lot of money for that skill. I'm also a pretty good actress. Now, you may not want to cast me, but I know one thing for damn sure—I'm not going to stand here and let you talk to me like this." And she left.

She landed the role of the Factory Girl . . . understudying Fantine. I'm sure, after she left the room, the notorious one said to his colleagues, "I like her. She's spunky. Did you see her standing up to me?" Or something like that. Who the hell knows?

The point is, every once in a while—very, very, very rarely—you may have to stand up for yourself. And when faced with abuse, you have every right to do so. Here's what Richard Dreyfuss has to say on the subject:

> There is such a common level of abuse given to the people who are being interviewed. It's necessary—it's so important—to turn around to the person who is interviewing you and tell them to go to hell . . . You have to let a creep know when he's being a creep. What happens to actors is that they are treated as talking pieces of meat, who have no other privilege than to act . . . And the fact of the matter is that the overwhelming majority of actors are smarter than the overwhelming majority of the people who are interviewing. So what happens is, after a while, you're being talked to as if you're not there. You're just the body sitting in the chair. You have to say, "Excuse me. I'd rather not do this job if this is what I have to go through." And there's a very specific reason why you do that. It's not just

because you want to be a bad guy or a rebel. But very simply: An actor's instrument is himself. And the more you give away . . . the less you have as an actor. Because your soul, your body, is your instrument.

So you have to always take the risk . . . You are not giving yourself away, you are not letting yourself be abused, and you are protecting what you have . . . It doesn't make sense to be humble and to be begging and pleading, because that means you are hurting your own work. And eventually, if you do get the part . . . you are not going to have enough resources to play the role.[10]

I hasten to add this absolutely crucial admonition: be very careful that you're not *inventing* the rudeness in your mind; that you're not misinterpreting some innocent remark or facial expression as some sort of abuse. Some of us move through our careers in a state of hypervigilance, springloaded and ready to pounce on just about anything and call it disrespect. There was a guy in one of my workshops in New York who reported, "I know what you mean about asshole casting directors. I was on this one audition, and after I finished my song, the casting director looked at me and said, 'Thank you so much for coming in.' You know? Like, 'Thank you for coming in.' I could tell she was like, 'You wasted your time and mine, so thanks a lot.'" And I was glad we were in such a huge group, because this actor got a

---

[10] Quoted from an interview in *How to Audition* by Gordon Hunt. Used with permission.

reality check that night. A roomful of fellow actors gently persuaded him to rethink his version of the story, because "Thank you so much for coming in" isn't an insult!

At another workshop an actress asked me, "How long do you tolerate disrespect? This one casting director has called me in *eighteen times* and never once called me back. Should I just stop going in?" How on earth do you turn eighteen auditions into "disrespect" in a business where those opportunities are so difficult to get? That's a huge compliment!

Some of you get thrown off if the people behind the table are talking to each other during your scene or song, or reading your resume instead of looking at you. I assure you, except in very rare cases, they're not being rude; they're just doing their work. I know an artistic director who is always on his computer during auditions. Know why? He's taking notes on the performers so he can remember them better. If you saw that and got insulted, you'd be 100% wrong.

So take note, and heed this warning well—don't automatically trust your perceptions when it comes to this one. Always give your auditors the benefit of the doubt, and unless there is blatant, obvious disrespect or abuse, assume you've totally imagined it. Because you probably have. While there's a great case to be made for taking a stand for your dignity, it doesn't pay to be a hothead, or paranoid, or oversensitive, or unrealistically and unreasonably demanding. I know far too many actors who, in misguided attempts to protect their dignity, have made taking offense into a lifestyle. They're really no fun to be around, because they're in a constant state of being indignant. Don't be inclined toward interpreting things that way. And if you are, *learn* that you have that inclination as quickly as possible. It falls to you to know the difference between disrespect and *imagined* disrespect. Otherwise you might just turn into a real jerk with whom no one wants to work.

Setting the Tone

Regardless of the personalities of the casting people you meet throughout your career, you can help them by simply entering their offices as a colleague and treating them as friendly collaborators (even if they're not so friendly). There's no need to timidly await a signal that will tell you how to behave. Often, you can set—or even change—the tone in the room. You have that kind of authority. Make the decision to establish a comfortable rapport right off the bat.

My friend Chane't Johnson is no longer with us. There isn't enough room, nor are there the proper words, to adequately convey all that was marvelous, brilliant, and lovely about this irresistible force of a woman. Among many other things, she was a badass actor, director, audition coach, and producer. Once, Chane't, who was a big black woman, went to audition for a role that was written for a skinny white woman. The talented casting director G. Charles Wright (who has great taste in actors and isn't afraid to be creative) knew Chane't would be a brilliant choice. The character lived her life by the TV show *Sex and the City*. Her motto was WWCBD—"What Would Carrie Bradshaw Do?" (Carrie Bradshaw was *Sex and the City*'s leading character. She and her friends were young, fun, hip, stylish New York women who had all sorts of adventures.) So Chane't got all dolled up, did her hair, put on her heels, and went to the audition. Instead of waiting for the room to approve of her, she walked in and casually cooed, "What up, sexy bitches?" She more or less had the part right then and there. Who could resist her?[11]

Here's one of the weirdest things I'm going to tell you. As you change your thinking on this whole process—your interpretation, your focus, all the stuff we've been talking about throughout this book—the atmosphere in casting rooms you enter will automatically change. You start to bring a certain vibe into the room with you that says "Hi there. Professional actor here. Everybody relax. I got this." It doesn't happen by trying to fake it, force it, or think up clever things to say. It happens because you've redefined what auditions are all about. You're no longer there to try to get people to hire you, like you, or legitimize you. You're now there to take care of them, put them at ease, and see whether you can help *them*. I think you're going to be surprised by the extent to which this new approach is going to change the kind of reception you get.

Another Mantra

It occurs to me that some of you may feel confused by what may sound like conflicting advice about our interactions with casting people. "They're mostly nice, but be prepared to stand up to those who aren't, but don't be paranoid, but

---

[11] Note: Despite speculation to the contrary, "What up, sexy bitches?" is not a magical incantation that hypnotizes casting people into hiring you. Don't be superstitious.

protect your own process, but take care of them?" Here's a code of conduct that brings all of these ideas together.

In the course of my career, I've encountered a fair number of stars (as well as some lesser-knowns who've exuded the poise and power of stardom). And I've noticed that, while most of these people are among the most likeable folks you could ever hope to meet, no one messes with them, and they're usually treated with respect. And I began to ponder, as I'm inclined to do, what goes on psychologically in that situation. How is this dynamic established? These people aren't intimidating; they're warm and gentle. And yet, something about their demeanor keeps you on your best behavior. How do they do that? And that pondering led me to a wonderful two-word answer: gracious strength.

That's the quality. The people who embody it can simultaneously make you feel like you're the only person in the room and also let you know you're in the presence of someone of substance. I once met the late, great actress Anne Bancroft. It was backstage after a performance of *The Producers*. I didn't want to miss the opportunity to express my admiration. "Ms. Bancroft," I said, "I'm Michael Kostroff. I'm in the cast, and I just want to say—" "Oh, I know who you are," she cooed warmly, knocking the breath out of my chest, "I've been enjoying your work." Her eyes connected with mine, and she gave me the hugest smile ever. I more or less don't remember what came next. She was generous and powerful all at once. A member of the cast of *The West Wing* once told me that when he met a certain President of the United States, he found him to be so focused on whomever he was talking to, and so engrossed in the conversation, that his aides had to pull him away for important presidential business. And how do actors of this ilk approach their interactions with the wide scope of personalities and temperaments they encounter throughout their careers? They exude gracious strength.

Jason Alexander, a personal friend as well as a guy I look up to more than I can say, was once in rehearsal with a director who didn't seem to grasp Jason's prestige and experience. The director tried to dictate Mr. Alexander's every gesture, line reading, and facial expression. It was insulting. But Jason didn't throw his weight around or act like a diva, nor did he kowtow and allow himself to be demeaned. With his irresistibly sunny smile, he walked over to the director, placed a loving hand on his shoulder, and said jokingly, "You know . . . I've done this a time or two before." They both laughed and Jason was treated with appropriate respect from that moment on.

There's a far more famous story about the legendary, Academy Award-winning actress Shelley Winters. Late in her career, with two Oscars and probably eighty films under her belt, a young director had the gall to ask her to come in for an audition. (Usually, stars—particularly legends like Ms. Winters—are simply offered films. They don't audition.) But Winters loved to work, so she went to see the young man. She sat down and immediately pulled an Oscar out of her enormous bag and plopped it down on his desk. Then she pulled out her second Oscar and plopped it down next to the first. "Still want me to audition?" she was reported to have asked. Wisely, the director withdrew his request and cast her in the film. She diffused an insult with humor while making a crystal clear statement about who she was.

Gracious strength is a quality I've decided to cultivate in my own career, another in my collection of mantras. I often—*often*—miss the mark. But I think it's an excellent goal for us. It's calmly saying, when someone is yelling, "Oh, let's not do that. I'm confident we can work it out without raising our voices, don't you think?" (instead of "Don't talk to me that way, asshole. I'm a professional," or worse, "Yes, sir. I'm sorry. I'll get it right."). It's processing unreasonable requests—like being handed a new audition scene and asked to perform it immediately—with a warm smile and a firm "Oh no, I don't think that's going to work for me. I'm just going to step out and study this scene for a few minutes. I think that will be best for all of us." *That's* gracious strength.

It's also knowing when to let someone's less-than-charming behavior pass without comment. Some people just aren't as classy as you are. Think of them as recent transplants from a country with very different customs and just let it go. That's part of being a mature professional. When you really own your value and dignity, you may have fewer instances in which you need to defend it.

Study the behavior of stars. Obviously, they're not all nice, but the ones with that classy, old-school grace are role models for us all. You don't need to be a celebrity, or even successful, to practice this kind of behavior. You just have to start thinking, "What would a big, classy star like Jennifer Lopez, Bryan Cranston, Meryl Streep, Viola Davis, Tom

Hanks, George Clooney, Morgan Freeman, Dustin Hoffman, Judy Dench . . . whomever . . . do in this situation?"

It's something to think about and revisit as you go along in your career. And it's a great approach to interacting with your auditors.

Now let's discuss some of the *not*-so-great approaches to interacting with your auditors . . .

Stop Doing That

We actors can be prone to engage in some very strange behavior once we cross the threshold into the audition room. We often present ourselves in ways that we think will ingratiate us to the casting director but, in fact, do the opposite. It's time to pick these behaviors apart . . . and cut them out.

- Don't gush.
  If you've been nervously pouring out oceans of compliments about the casting director's office, hairstyle, recent projects, or charming personality, please stop. I promise you, for most people, being on the receiving end of that kind of unbridled praise is creepy and uncomfortable.

  To illustrate this point, one of the things I started doing in my workshops is asking to interview a girl who gets hit on a lot. I question my volunteers about their reactions to various approaches from men. Their answers have been remarkably consistent. Every one of them has told me that the guy who approaches with gushing flattery, telling her how amazing she is, falling all over himself to praise her, treating her like she's some sort of magically angelic and intimidatingly sexy alien creature isn't the guy she wants to go out with. In fact, she really, really doesn't want to go out with him in any way. When asked what kind of approach they *would* respond to positively, these women describe a guy who has a sense of his own value (without being arrogant) and expresses interest (without desperately trying to ingratiate himself).

I believe it's the same for casting folks. When you slather them with compliments, it can be a real turn-off. It could also make them feel manipulated, and no one likes that. So the lesson is simple: be nice, be normal, and don't be creepy. (There's one for your index card.)

- Don't grovel.
  As I said at the beginning of this chapter, there is no reason to treat the people in the audition room like members of the All-Powerful High Court of Show Business Rejection. These folks represent your potential collaborators. Remember that. That's who you're meeting: people who work for the people you might be working with. There's absolutely no reason to abase yourself like a lowly beggar, as if it's a humbling, undeserved privilege merely to be in the same room. Just show your carpet samples like a dignified pro and get on with your day.

- Don't ask permission, and don't apologize.

  I really want you to think about these two things. We actors have a terrible habit of behaving like inept little servants. We're told it's our turn to audition, and yet we'll still tap timidly on the door, poke our heads in, and ask if we should come in, then apologize for not knowing the protocol. We fumble with the door, and apologize. We ask whether it's OK to use a chair for the audition, then, if we're told, "I think it's better if you stand," we'll say, "Oops! Sorry." Cut that out. These are overly subservient tics that position us again and again as people who don't deserve to be in the room.

  If you want to sit for the scene, just sit. You don't have to ask. You're the expert. Make your presentation the way you, as the expert, have decided to make it. If the casting person says she'd prefer that you stand, *don't apologize!* What the hell are you sorry for? "It's better for the camera if you stand for this." "Great!" And stand up. Look at that. You've already been able to give the casting person something she wants. What a pro!

  What is it about us actors that makes us so fucking apologetic? I'm baffled by this. We've come in to help people accomplish their casting goals. We're offering them our artistic abilities. This is a *gift*, not an imposition. We're not beggars. We're helpers. We need to stop being so sorry all the time.

Because, just as no one wants to deal with a nervous person, no one wants to deal with a person who feels he has a lot to be sorry for. Whether one realizes it or not, habitual apologizing puts the casting person in the exhausting position of having to repeatedly reassure actors that everything is fine.

The same is true for asking permission. Asking "Do you mind if I wear my glasses?" "Should I start now?" "Can I sit?" isn't the behavior of a professional, and it makes more work for the casting director, who is now answering questions about how you should do your work! When the dentist comes in, you want him to bloody well know what he wants to do, what tools to use, and how to use them. You don't want him asking permission. It simply doesn't inspire confidence.

- Knock off the self-effacing jokes.
  One thing that's not nearly as appealing as we think is self-effacing humor—putting ourselves down or making jokes at our own expense. I'm not sure why, but this seems to be a go-to for actors. We think that's adorable. It isn't. I once watched a wonderful, superbly talented actress do this to herself. The director asked, "Can you try this with a German accent?" and she said something like, "Well, I guess we'll find out. Probably not a <u>good</u> one. Brace yourselves, everyone!" And she chuckled, and so did the director. She then proceeded to perform the scene with a flawless German accent. After she walked

out, I asked him, "Does that bother you, when actors do that?" "Yes," he said. "She's telling me she may not be able to play the role, and that makes me uneasy." The humor that puts yourself down is needy and desperate, and it doesn't serve you. So stop it.

I know why we do it. Again, we're very concerned that people might perceive us as arrogant if we don't demonstrate an incredibly humble opinion of ourselves. For most actors, that's not something to be worried about. Most of us, as I've said, are in far greater danger of coming across as lowly beggars who are expecting to be dismissed posthaste to make room for more talented candidates. It's not an appealing impression.

Yes, there are some of you out there—*some*—who may indeed need to address a tendency to come across as smug, self-satisfied, or arrogant. And it's important to learn whether you're in that minority. For you, the answer will not be to put yourselves down with self-effacing jokes but, rather, to work harder at showing deep interest in any input from the person running the session. I have one wildly talented friend who told me she always has to leave something for the casting director to "fix" because, she said, "When you bring mastery before those who don't understand it, they don't recognize what it is, and therefore may resent it." And so she holds off on blowing them out of the water until they've had a chance to make a suggestion or two, to which she responds with tremendous gratitude.

You know what I think we peddle, ultimately, as auditioning actors, more than anything else? Wrapped around our acting skills and our suitability for a given role, I believe we peddle a sense of security. That's what we need to be able to offer. When a casting person calls you back, he or she is, in essence, saying to the producer and director, "I think this actor is good for this part." We need to reassure the people making that unspoken statement that we won't embarrass them in any way, and that we'll make them look like smart casting people for finding such a solid, poised, competent actor. And the same is true at the next phase of the process. When a director chooses you for a role, he wants to know that you're a safe choice, that you'll make his job easier, not harder, by delivering the goods, being comfortable and not needy, and remaining calm. So I think, when you're auditioning, you need to let the people in the room know that you've got things covered—that, should they decide to cast you, everything will be OK, because you're on it; they're in the hands of a pro. We need to offer that kind of security at the very first audition. Way down deep inside, you *know* you can handle the job. So present yourself accordingly. Otherwise, it's like placing an exquisite, imported, gourmet, twelve-layer, dark-chocolate-hazelnut-marzipan-mocha-buttercream torte in a greasy, warped, beat-up box. It's hard to trust the product when the presentation is dodgy.

We close out this chapter with observations from some of the very people we've been discussing. Here are casting directors, sharing their take on actors' biggest misconceptions about who they are and what they do. You may detect some patterns:

I think many actors have difficulty believing that we are on their side. We want actors to succeed. We want actors to do well and be happy. We admire their courage, the sacrifices they make to be artists. —Tara Rubin

I feel like actors don't always realize that I want to interact, and I really want all of the actors to do a great job. I am having auditions because I need to cast actors in roles. —Alison Franck

There's a misconception people have that we know what we're looking for. We don't. We're hoping for someone to have the answers and help us figure it out. —James Calleri

I suppose it's a cliché to say, "We're on their side," but—really— we're on their side! Also, there are a lot of commonalities between casting directors and actors: we're all hustling for our next job and, though it might seem that our lives are more stable, that is definitely not always the case. —Michael Cassara

[The biggest misconception about casting directors is] probably that we are scary people! We want actors to do well. —Shakyra Dowling

They forget that we are human too. Also, we are rooting for the actor. We want each actor to have a fantastic audition so we can get the roles cast! We also go through just as many ups and downs as actors. We wonder where our next job is coming from. We sometimes have bad days and still have to put on a brave face, be present, and do our job. Just like actors have to do! —Jami Rudofsky

[A] common misconception is that [casting] is an easy and powerful job. It is definitely fun . . . But it is not easy and it is not powerful. Ultimately we are only there to influence the director's decision . . . and don't have the power to cast an actor. —Shruti Mahajan

I tell them and tell them not to take it personally, that the way a director picks an actor is like falling in love—it's an unexplainable spark. —Tina Buckingham

Some of the biggest misconceptions are:

1) *That casting directors choose the cast. We do not choose the cast. We lead, administer, and facilitate the casting process. We make recommendations. We develop actors. We shape talent. We collaborate with our creative teams to help them create their vision.*

2) *That we have some kind of "power" over actors. Actors don't realize that they have all the power in the room. Sure, we decide if they get a callback in the early stages; but that's about where it ends. But the moment they walk into the room, that room is theirs to command. To inspire. To create. To shape. To tell the story. And if we fall in love with them we are so happy when the actor says yes; and so, so sad when they say no.*

3) *I think actors forget that we have to fight for the jobs too. Casting is a tremendously competitive and very small industry. Like any industry, the 1% get 99% of the high-profile jobs. So the rest of us have to find ways to stand out, just like actors do.*

4) *The "adversarial relationship" issue. It may be helpful for actors to think of us as comrades rather than gate-keepers. We are all in this together. A CD's job is tremendously stressful and time-consuming. There is a ton of pressure on us to deliver what the client wants; and often, they don't know what they want until we show them. That's where so much of our creativity comes into play. So actors must learn to trust us, trust the process, and know that when we say "no" to them that it's not personal. I can't stand when I hear an actor say "[insert CD's name here] HATES me. I just never get anywhere with her." It's not about you. It's about one artist using our judgment to put together a group of artists that we think the team will respond to, and to give them choices. We know what we are doing. You don't. Trust us, trust the process, and have some human empathy for the people behind the table.*
—Joy Dewing

CHAPTER TEN

T-T-TALKING

O K. Sometimes, before you get to read the scene, the casting person or director will want to chat with you a bit. Now, this part is already going to go better than it has for you in the past because now, you're not there to beg or be needy or to get it "right," you're there to take care of them—to put *them* at ease. But to make this go even more smoothly, I have two sneaky techniques to teach you.

1) Give simple pleasant answers—not necessarily accurate ones. I have a tendency to be an accuracy freak. Ask me how I am and I may launch into a full analysis of the highs and lows, making sure I've given a precise account of the full spectrum of my state of being, rather than offering the simple pleasant answer "Great!" It used to be that people would say, "So, Michael, you're from New York?" And I'd say, "Well, originally, yes, but my

family moved a few times. We lived in Florida for four years, and then I've been back and forth between New York and L.A. . . . " Ugh. Wake me when it's over. This is *not* an interesting story. So now when someone asks whether I'm from New York, I just say, "Yep! Born and raised." And we all move on. Don't waste time giving in-depth, detailed answers. No one will fact-check you after you leave the room, unless you're claiming credits and connections you don't have. Give simple, pleasant answers—not necessarily accurate ones.

2)   Answer the question you wish they'd asked. This is a goodie. You'll see politicians do this one a lot. They'll be asked, "What about the economy?" and they'll answer, "I'm glad you asked that. Because you know, everything stems back to education. The education of our children is our most important investment . . . " And we're onto the topic of education, and off the economy.

As I write this, I'm recurring on the series *Luke Cage*. If I'm meeting with a TV casting director, I might want to be sure to mention the show, because it's current and it's a series.

But what if he doesn't ask about that? What if he's a big musical theatre fan, and asks, "Oh! You were in *Les Mis*? What was that like?" I find a way to answer the question I wish he'd asked, like so: "Oh it was great! Of course, I have no time for theatre these days. Since I'm on *Luke Cage* this season, I'm spending most of my time at the studio." See how clever this little technique is? I've just sneakily changed the subject.

"Hey, Michael. I like that shirt. Where did you get it?" "You know, it's so funny you should ask. It's my lucky shirt. I wore it to my audition for *Luke Cage* and now I'm filming the series!" Is it my lucky shirt? Of course not. Do we care? Of course not.

What if you want the casting director to know you've worked with the director before? "How've you been?" "Great! I love that Elizabeth is directing this project. She's such a talented woman." What if you have knowledge of the piece? "How are you?" "Excited! I've read this book several times and always thought it would make a great film."

You should all start practicing this right away. Instead of hoping people ask the right questions, you can guide them to your preferred topic.

I'll add this for balance. Many actors get it in their heads that providing certain information is going to make a difference in the casting director's decision. That can get a bit desperate. It doesn't track logically. Think about it. No one is going to give you a callback or a role because you've worked with a particular director, or read a particular book, or because you've been cast in something else. The value of answering the question you wish they'd asked isn't to stack the deck in your favor; it's to help you feel less like you're taking a test and more like a participant in the conversation. Make sense?

Now sometimes, a casting person will ask whether you have questions about the material before you read. It's a nice courtesy. But I've been surprised to learn, through teaching my workshop, that some actors have anxiety about it. Let me alleviate your concerns. First of all, it's OK not to have any questions. In fact, it's sexy. I usually have no questions about my audition materials. And I usually see a glint in the casting person's eye that says, "Got it. You're a pro." Sometimes you do have questions, and that's great too. That shows you've studied the material and you know what information you need to do your work.

However, there are questions that are appropriate and others that are not. Any specific question about something that will affect how you perform the material you're about to perform is appropriate, as long as it doesn't ask the casting person to do your work for you. Here are some examples of great questions. "How do you pronounce this word?" "I'm not clear. Is the character lying here, or does she really believe what she's saying?" And what are the inappropriate questions? Well, they fall into two categories, but they're both compensations for nerves and insecurity. In the first, you show that you don't trust your own expertise by asking, "Do you want this with an accent?" "How big do you want this?" or worst of all, "How do you see this character?" or "How do you want this played?" Once again, those questions throw obligations onto the other person, the person who is looking to you for your help and expertise. All those things are your job.

A true painter doesn't ask people how they want him to create his paintings. He does his art. People buy it or they don't. You're an artist. By definition, it's your individual expression that you're charged with sharing. Don't weaken that expression by offering someone a blank canvas and handing him a brush.

But look, acting is a nuanced thing. There may be occasions when a discussion of character is called for. At those times, you should ignore my advice, recognize that you're the expert, and do your thing in the way that works for you.

The second category of inappropriate questions is those that have nothing to do with the audition. "Yeah, when does this film? Because I know I have a bar mitzvah I'm going to on the 21st. But, I mean, I can miss it if I need to." No one has asked you to do the role. And they're not going to. You don't need to know when it's filming. Because when it does, it will be without you. What have I been telling you all along? You're not getting the fucking job! Here are some other bad questions. "Yeah, who's in the cast?" "Are you seeing a lot of people for the part?" "Do you think I'm right for this, type-wise?" We usually ask questions like these just to create conversation or to postpone doing the scene. Asking nonpertinent questions wastes time and creates discomfort. Your job is to create comfort.

CHAPTER ELEVEN

PERFORMANCE ANXIETY

Well, here we are. It took us almost a whole book to get here, but we're finally at the main event—the part where you get to perform. And true to my promise at the beginning of this book, I'm not going to teach you a single bloody thing about acting (not on purpose, anyway). Instead, we're going to take a look at what's happening psychologically *while* you're performing, and how we can make that part a lot better. Let's start with some don'ts:

- As much as possible, avoid doing any elaborate preparations in the room. It really weirds people out. The funny sketch-comedy cliché is the overly serious actor in a black turtleneck who says, "I'll need a moment to prepare," turns around, lowers his head, does a series of vocal warm-ups, followed by some calisthenics, stretches, head rolls, more vocal exercises, then, finally, turns around with an intense, far-away look in his eye, and delivers his audition: "What time does the bus leave?" Then he comes out of his technique-induced trance, as if he's just done the complete works of Shakespeare, and intones grandly, "and . . . scene."

If you need a few transitional seconds, by all means take them. Don't announce them. Just take them. But for the most part, you should do your preparation work before you cross the threshold.

- Remember: don't ask permission, and don't apologize. Present your work in the way that seems best to you, the expert, and do so with dignity, and with the authority of the professional acting consultant you are. We're wonderful, creative beings who can do magic. Stop groveling.

- Don't rush. Take your time. You don't score points at an audition by performing the material faster than anyone else. What are you trying to do, go for the record? Rushing communicates something along the lines of, "Nothing to see here. I'll just make this quick and get out of your hair. I'm sure you have more important things to do." Taking your time says, "You might want to take a look at this. There's something going on here that's worth noting. It takes up a bit of space, and it earns it." Now, is there such a thing as taking too much of your time? Oh, you bet your ass there is. Indulgent, pause-heavy auditions are obnoxious, and usually a bit calculated. Act the scene at a pace appropriate to the material. Give it space. Allow your character to breathe and think and process. But don't let things drag just for effect.

- I want to also discourage you from asking if you can start the scene again. Here's what every casting director I know says about that. About 100% of the time, the second reading will be exactly like the first. To everyone but you. You'll think, "Ah, yes. Much better. That's how I meant to do it." But for those who are watching, it's pretty much the same as before you interrupted yourself. So all you will have done is create unease and demonstrate a lack of professional self-assurance. Don't do it. Don't ask if you can start again. See, actors think that if they blow a word, or don't deliver a line exactly as planned, they've blown the audition. Dumb. Casting people are looking at other things. Words can be learned. They want a sense of what kind of actor you are and your overall version of the character.

If you absolutely must, must, must start again—like if you've had a huge coughing fit mid-scene that obscured a whole page of dialogue—then *don't ask,* just do it. Say, "I'm going to start again," and don't wait for permission. Just do it. But please, please listen to my advice on this, and don't start again just because you don't like how the scene is going.

- Don't be afraid to be brilliant. If you have a wonderful performance in you, don't shrink from it. Don't apologize for it. Don't seek permission to share it. This might sound odd to most of you, but I suspect it will make great sense for a few of you. Your own talent can be a big and scary thing, and sometimes we're not sure it's OK to let it out of the box.

I believe that true performers are born different. We come into this world like little flames. We think differently. And many of us are born into families of "Muggles" who don't understand us. So we grow up hearing, "What's wrong with you?" "Why do you have to be so loud?" "What are you wearing?" "Why do you have to walk like that?" "Talk like a normal person," and even, as I did, "Who do you think you are? You're no one special."

And so we learn to tamp down what's flamboyant and wild and lovely and unique about us. We learn not to be too big or too different; we try to blend. We don't want people to think we think we're anything special. But when you're performing—and remember, that's what an audition is, a chance to perform—you don't have to hide your beautiful gifts. You don't have to be less than you are. This is the world you were made for, where your ability to morph into other people, or your funny voices, or your loud singing, is welcomed, encouraged, and understood. So if you have a brilliant take on a role, or a scene, or a song, bring that shit. And don't hold back. You've only got one performance.

I once heard a speaker say this (sadly, I can't seem to remember who it was, but he made a great point). Ask a kid, he said, "Can you sing?" "Yes." Can you dance?" "Yes." "Can you act?" "Yes, and I can speak Spanish and play flute and do impressions." Because they can do all those things. They're not evaluating their proficiency or rating themselves against others. It's only when we get older that we start to say, "Well . . . I'm not a *singer* singer. Not like Pavarotti or anything." "I dance OK, but I'm not like a ballet dancer."

It's true that, as professionals, we do need to have a realistic assessment of our work and what we can offer, and at what level, but I think we have to watch the weird magnetic pull toward undervaluing. Undervaluing is no more realistic than overvaluing. And if you decide to go in and audition, you really need to leave all that crap behind. Those critical voices from your childhood don't serve you, and neither does comparing your work with the work of others. Your offerings, however meager, are the only ones you have to offer. Bring them, give them, and share them fully.

- And the biggest don't of all, which merits its own subheading . . .

Don't Watch It, *Do* It

Perhaps the greatest enemy of good auditioning is self-evaluation. Attempting to watch or listen to yourself *while* you're playing your scene or singing your song and evaluate how you're doing is a total performance killer. It yanks you right out of the world of the character and makes you too self-conscious to do good work. It's also a devilishly hard habit to break. So this is a point worth dwelling on, because many of us fall into this trap of trying to watch ourselves audition and track how it's going, which is very much like turning around really fast to look at a mirror in the hopes of seeing the back of your head.

When I was young and skinny and had all my hair, I often auditioned for the role of Che in *Evita*. For the four of you who don't know the plot, here it is in a nutshell: Eva Peron claws her way to the top by questionable means and becomes the First Lady of Argentina. Che Guevara appears as a fantasy character, damning her and bitterly mocking those who fall for her act. Inevitably, auditions for Che involve singing the song "High Flying Adored," in which he exposes the irony of this glorified guttersnipe being worshiped like royalty. The highest note in the song is a G, which, back then, was really high for me. The first two Gs came on the lyric, "Were there *stars* in your eyes when you crawled in at night, from the *bars*, from the sidewalk, from the gutter theatrical?" And whenever I knew that friggin' note was coming up, I started to prepare myself to try to hit it. And guess what happened? I cracked. Or I was flat. Or it just sounded like shit. I tried all kinds of ways to hit that fucking G—imagining it was lower, using pure muscle, screaming—it wasn't good.

One day, while waiting to audition, I made a decision. I decided I that was not going to sing any Gs that day. Instead, I was going to demand answers from Eva Peron, to make her account for herself, to accuse her without apology. And guess what happened? Gs for days. Beautiful, rich, soaring Gs that could have bored into the very soul of that Argentine bitch.

(By the way, this is a great thing for you singers out there to learn: composers often write the higher notes to express higher emotions. Most often, you'll find there are important things the character wants to—no, *has* to—say. When Jean Valjean, the hero of *Les Misérables*, declares his true identity, it's a high note. "Who am I? 24601!" In the famous musical theatre anthem "You'll Never Walk Alone," the highest note is on the word "*ne*ver." It's the same reason that songs sometimes modulate—the key change raises the emotional climate, making the ideas more important. So if you have high notes to sing, focus on the *intention*, not the notes.)

When you go on an audition, you have something important to do, but it isn't to book a job or impress a casting person. If you're Che Guevara, you have to get an answer out of Eva Peron. If you're Hamlet, you have to decide, in that very moment, whether "To be, or not to be" (a pretty big task). You might have to figure out how to "solve a problem like Maria," or get that damned spot out. You might be a doctor who must tell a patient that the test results are inconclusive, or a mother who needs to get the kids inside for dinner, or a guy at a bar who needs to persuade a girl to come home with him, or a gossip who has *got* to get the latest dish. If you're the jury forewoman, you have to tell the judge the verdict or he won't know what it is. There's no time to assess your performance or try to get an acting job. You have work to do!

And that mindset, I promise you, is like a magical raft that sails you gently over the thrashing waves. Really take on the character's need, the character's desire, what he wants to find out, or communicate, or achieve, and the only nerves or anxieties you'll experience will be the character's. Dive in deep, and you'll find there's no more room for your actor problems. I once coached a friend who was auditioning for the dual role of Miss Gulch and The Wicked Witch of the West in *The Wizard of Oz*. "Neither Miss Gulch nor The Wicked Witch give a shit about this audition, or being liked, or standing out," I told her. "You don't need to do any of those things. You have only two tasks: get the fucking dog; get the fucking shoes."

Now doesn't that sound like a lot more fun?

I was a serious devotee of the TV singing competition show *American Idol*. People knew not to call me when it was on. I'd dial in to vote for my favorite contestants. And after the episode in which Jennifer Hudson was voted off, six friends called to ask if I was OK. I couldn't discuss it.

Seriously, I think every actor should watch performance competition shows like *American Idol*, because they're nothing but a series of auditions. And there's a lot to be learned. Putting talent aside for a moment, I want you to take a look at the contestants' demeanor. There are some who are very conscious of their singing, hoping not to botch things. That's not your "idol." Then there are those with confidence, who sing well, and know how to deliver a song. OK. They're good. But then there's Fantasia Barrino. You have to go back and watch some of her performances and study them with the ideas of this book in mind. When Fantasia comes out, she has something important that she has to tell you. *Has* to. And here's the thing. *She is not auditioning for you.* She is there to tell you something, or share a feeling, or tell a story. That's what she's doing. Not hoping you'll like her. Not trying to win a contest. She makes the song important to her. And suddenly, you're in Fantasialand. You're on *her* turf. And it's completely compelling. The same is true for Adam Lambert, Jennifer Hudson, and several others, though they're not always the winners. (Don't get me started.) Watch their faces. They're not evaluating themselves. They're doing their thing. They're in it.

Even more than competition shows, I urge you to watch a documentary called *Every Little Step.* It's about the auditions for the revival of *A Chorus Line.* I especially want you to watch Jason Tam's audition for the role of Paul. The auditors had been hearing the same monologue all day long, performed beautifully by professionals. But when Mr. Tam delivered it, these seasoned vets behind the table found themselves welling up, wiping away tears, speechless. It was fresh, because he let the moments *happen* to him. He let himself experience the scene. He never seemed to be competing, evaluating, trying to impress, trying to get it right, or trying to get a job. Instead, he—as Paul—seemed to *need* the people listening to understand the story he was sharing, and as a result, the performance was irresistible.

Let me put it another way. We're on page number 146, we've spent some time together, we've gotten to know each other, and I think it's time for the next step in our relationship. So let's talk about sex.

If you're in the midst having sex . . . and you're thinking about how it's going . . . you're not having sex. You're missing it. And I'm sorry if this weirds you out, but I don't think it's too much of a stretch to say that an audition ought to be like good sex. Don't you want to get completely lost in it? Don't you want the room to go away? Shouldn't it be almost sensual? Don't you want that feeling where you're all wrapped up in it and it all washes over you and carries you along? Wow! I want that! You don't get there by thinking, "I'm going to put my hand over here. That'll really be good. Ooh, she seems to like that . . . uh-oh, I don't think that worked . . . " Ugh! Let go, actors. Relish the experience. Get lost in the scene. Let it swirl around you. And leave the evaluating to those who do that for a living.

I had a breakthrough in this department while shooting an episode of *The Closer*. I played one of two doctors who had accidentally killed a kid on the operating table, then covered it up. There was this long interrogation room scene in which the other doctor had most of the lines. And as I sat there, listening, instead of being the actor trying to act well, I just let myself be the doctor. And I found myself thinking, "How did I end up in an interrogation room? I'm a respected doctor. How can I live with myself? Even if I don't go to jail, I'm going to give up medicine. We don't kill people. This isn't why I got into this profession. What am I going to tell my wife?" I forgot the cameras were there, and experienced the grief and remorse I imagined this character would feel. In the final edit, the director chose to include lots of shots of me, just sitting there, thinking, experiencing, deep in the world of the scene, where there were no cameras or lights, no script, no need to impress anyone.

It's not your line readings or facial expressions or carefully planned gestures that make casting people think you might be a good choice for a role; it's the overall essence of your characterization—the person you're bringing to life before their eyes. They won't say, "Let's bring back that woman who paused and pointed her finger on that line." They'll say, "Let's bring back that woman who seemed to be really living it." So stop doing that "auditioning acting." Play the character. Enact the story. Surrender to the experience, and stop watching yourself.

Here's a great quote about not evaluating your gift. It was written by the legendary, groundbreaking choreographer Martha Graham to the legendary, groundbreaking choreographer Agnes De Mille.

> There is a vitality, a life force, a quickening that is translated through you into action, and because there is only one of you in all time, this expression is unique. If you block it, it will never exist through any other medium, and be lost. The world will not have it. It is not your business to determine how good it is; nor how valuable it is; nor how it compares with other expressions. It is your business to keep it yours, clearly and directly, to keep the channel open. You do not

> even have to believe in yourself or your work. You have to keep open and aware directly to the urges that motivate you. Keep the channel open. No artist is ever pleased. There is no satisfaction whatever at any time. There is only a queer, divine dissatisfaction; a blessed unrest that keeps us marching and makes us more alive than the others.[12]

Isn't that good? I especially like the part about there being no satisfaction, how we're never pleased. Man, that sounds like artists to me—forever trying to get it right when there is no right. There is no finished. There is no perfect. It's art. "No satisfaction whatever at any time. Only a queer, divine dissatisfaction." Accepting that—and getting away from self-evaluation and the fruitless act of comparing your art to that of others—makes it infinitely easier to just enjoy what you're able to do with your particular talents.

And by the way, there is nothing wrong with being aware of, and appreciating, your own abilities. That's not arrogance; that's healthy self-esteem and gratitude.

For years, I studied with a brilliant, highly accomplished voice teacher from whom I learned about far more than just singing. An extraordinary vocalist himself, he was a firm believer in the enjoyment of one's own gifts. One day, after a lesson, he said, "Hang on. I want to play something for

---

[12] Martha Graham, as quoted in *Dance to the Piper and Promenade Home* by Agnes de Mille (De Capo Press, 1982)

you." We went into his den, where he pressed PLAY and settled into his chair. It was a recording of him, singing. The sound was heavenly. But what was even more captivating and inspiring to me was watching him as he listened to himself sing. He was enraptured, eyes closed, a beaming, beatific smile on his face as he savored every note. After a bit, he stirred from his reverie and sighed with amazement, "Isn't that great?" Was this arrogance? Not at all. My teacher was enjoying what he was able to do with his voice, almost as an outsider would. And wouldn't it have been a terrible shame if he *couldn't* hear how beautiful his singing was on that recording?

I feel that way about being able to make people laugh. When I deliver a comedic moment in a way I think will be funny and hear an entire audience respond, I'm so excited by that ability. I'm happy that I have an instinct for comedy. That's not conceit at all; it's humbling, really. I just feel like I was given a gift that not everyone has, and I'm grateful for it. Look, friends: we're in a career with all too few payoffs. Don't cheat yourself by not enjoying what you're able to do.

Next time you see the film *Cabaret*, I want you to look for a particular moment I love. It's the scene where Michael York ("Cliff") sees Liza Minnelli ("Sally") perform for the first time. He's sitting in the club and she's on stage doing her Liza thing. She finishes the number to big applause and, moments later, we see her sitting at one of the tables. Michael York comes over and says, in his proper English accent, "You know you're really very good." And Liza, without missing a beat, replies, "Oh, I know, darling. Isn't it *marvelous*?"

It always astounds me how easy it is to let the joy of acting slip away and be replaced by this mythical thing called The Audition. When we audition, most of us have a bad habit of doing something *other* than what we do when we're working as actors. And so we're not enjoying our gifts, because we've sucked all the fun out of performing in our desire to "nail" it.

But we're going to work on that from now on, aren't we? So that means that when you audition, you're now free to find the truth in the scene or the song or the monologue, to play the moments, to experience the circumstances as if they're real. You're not going to concoct clever line readings or convincing facial expressions, you're going craft *performances*, and work on staying connected and honest and doing some real acting, even if the other lines are being read by an expressionless, unconvincing reader.

I have a term I love to use with regard to acting: "lift-off." You know that moment when a plane leaves the ground and you're flying? Well, acting can have lift-off too—even in a casting office. That's the moment when, instead of trying to manipulate or evaluate the scene, it's just happening. It's in flight, soaring through the air. I love when that happens. It can only come from getting completely off the idea of booking a gig and back into your job description: actor.

Go for lift-off. It's a wonderful feeling.

About Faces
Every bit as deadly as trying to evaluate yourself mid-performance is the foolhardy act of trying to assess what an

auditor is thinking while watching your work. Besides being absolutely the wrong focus, it's easy to misinterpret a facial expression.

You'll often hear actors say of a casting director, "Well . . . she *hated* me." They'll state it as a fact. Ask them, "How do you know?" "Oh, believe me, I could just tell. She was looking at me like, 'Why are you even here?'"

Hang on. Can you tell what people are thinking by looking at them?

One of the early challenges I faced as a teacher was resisting the urge to interpret the expressions on my students' faces. Trust me, if I had, I would have quit teaching. Many of them looked like they hated me. Some looked bored, some skeptical, some resentful, some not even present. I was always surprised when they returned after the mid-class break. Then, at the end of the class, those same people would come up, misty eyed, and thank me for changing their lives.

A casting director I once worked with sat expressionless, looking bored while an actress sung her heart out in a soaring ballad. After the actress left the room the casting director turned to me and said, "Isn't she fantastic?"

Now what accounts for this? Simple. When you're paying attention to something, you're not aware of your expression. You're not trying to control it. It's your mind that's engaged, not your facial muscles. Check yourself next time you're watching your favorite thrilling or hilarious

TV program. See what your face is doing. It's probably doing nothing at all. Or sneak a peek at a fellow moviegoer. Chances are you'll find you're sitting next to an expression-less zombie.

You know what I learned about me? When I'm learning choreography, my face looks like I hate it. I don't know why. Maybe the intense concentration (it's been a while since I danced regularly) reads like disapproval. But I've been stunned again and again by choreographers getting snippy with me all of a sudden. "What, Michael? What is it?" snapped one of them, "You don't like the choreography? You're looking at me like I'm an asshole." Well, I wasn't. I was just trying to learn the damn steps.

So, when a casting director is watching you audition, don't watch him back. He's not thinking about what his face is doing and neither should you. Don't write the story for your auditors. Don't decide what they're thinking. They might be scowling, but loving everything you're doing. They might be smiling, but thinking about lunch. Or they might just be processing whether you and the role are a potential match. Remember, that's their job.

What About . . . ?
Now, based on my experience, I'm guessing that right around now, many of you are starting to wonder about specific audition dos and don'ts. "I'm short. Is it OK to wear really high heels?" "Is it appropriate to mention that you've worked with the director?" "Can I wear my reading glasses?" "Do you recommend sending thank-you notes afterwards?" and so forth. I'm afraid you may find my

answer a little bit frustrating. Because my answer to any question you're having right now is going to be the same. Here it is: you are the expert. Start thinking like one. Decide for yourself.

Why do we ask whether it's OK to say or do certain things at auditions? It's because we have this idea that we are forever in danger of doing something inappropriate or offensive, as if we're meeting royalty and there is a time-honored set of protocols. And so we worry that, at any turn, we could commit an unforgivable faux pas and perhaps be sentenced to beheading. I suggest to you that it's not so dangerous as all that. It's not like that board game, Operation, where you have to try to remove plastic bones, and if you move too far in one direction, a loud, anxiety-inducing buzzer goes off. These are people you're meeting. You don't have to be so damned careful. You need glasses? Wear them. Or retype your sides in a larger font like I do. Own your expertise and your authority. And try to wean yourself off the idea that there's some endless minefield full of ways you might offend or make a bad impression. Getting rid of that insane mythology will have far more value than having me suggest specific behaviors for the audition room.

The Big Finish

When you reach the end of your performance, be sure to play out the last moment. Don't bail on the end of the scene. Stick the landing, as they say in gymnastics, then return your focus to the person for whom you're performing. Do it with authority. Hold your dignity, and the dignity of the work you've just done. Some of you finish a powerful scene, then shrug sheepishly as if to ask, "Was that OK?"

thereby throwing your own work right under the bus. Don't do anything that apologizes for or questions your performance.

You also don't need to ask whether they need to see you do anything else, or whether they have any notes. If they need something, they'll ask for it. Don't forget: you're the acting expert in the room. You're there to help *them*. So assume you've just given them a huge gift—one great choice for the role—and that your expertise is obvious and doesn't require a second chance to show itself. At the same time, they're the *casting* experts. So they don't need to be reminded that they can give you notes. They know that. So do your thing, and call it done. It's appropriate to say "thanks" before you go, but trust that they'll let you know if they need further help.

Adjustments

Now, sometimes, the person for whom you're auditioning will give you an "adjustment," as they usually call it these days. That's a note on how to play the scene, a direction. Here's what you *have* to know—an adjustment is always a compliment. Auditors don't give adjustments to people who have just done a terrible job of reading for a role. An adjustment means they like what you're doing and they want to see if you can do it a little differently. I know how you are. Some of you get an adjustment and instantly interpret it in the worst way possible. "Damn. I got it wrong." No you didn't. You got it right. So right, in fact, that the person doing the casting wants to collaborate with you and make it even more right. They want to spend more time with you. It's like being out on a dinner date and having the other person say, after the meal, "You know, I'm not tired yet. Let's go bowling!"

This is a great opportunity to demonstrate poise and professionalism. Make the casting person feel good about the adjustment. Every adjustment is a great adjustment, whether you think so or not. Never debate or discredit. If you need clarification, ask for it, in a positive, collaborative way. Believe it or not, somewhere in the world there's an actor who gets defensive and tries to poke holes in the logic of the adjustment (remember, actors are crazy). So be glad that's not you.

There's a psychological advantage to discussing the adjustment a bit, if such a discussion is called for: you are now demonstrating what it's like to work with you. You've created a collaboration that wasn't there a few moments earlier. You're now colleagues, working together on a project. Subconsciously, the casting person has now moved you into a different category. It's now started to feel a lot like a rehearsal and a lot less like an audition.

As you dive back into the scene with your new adjustment, don't get anxious about showing how different your second performance is from your first. Think about the verb "adjust." It's not "overhaul," "restructure," "throw everything out and start again," or "be completely different." Adjust. Unless the casting person's note involves something radically different from your original approach, just bend your interpretation enough to fold in the new direction. The casting person will be watching specifically for that, so even the subtlest shifts will show up in bold color. Sometimes, it won't feel as if you've changed anything, but just having the fresh thoughts in your brain will show up in your performance. And sometimes, the casting person will believe they see the adjustment even if you've done nothing.

It's not a test. There is no passing or failing. You aren't going to get the fucking job. So think of it as an extension of your chance to act on a Thursday.

CHAPTER TWELVE

POSTMORTEM

OK. The audition is over. You prepared, you picked out an outfit, you went somewhere, you went in, and you did your thing. Now what? Well, I think you know what I'm going to say. You're not getting the fucking job. There's no job. So why are you still thinking about it? Some actors like to ask their agents to ask for feedback. Feedback is useful if you're a beginner and aren't sure whether you can act. Otherwise, the only feedback you'll need is whether you've booked the job. That's not going to happen. So let it go.

You will always give your best performance . . . in the car on the way home. Or on the subway, metro, cable car, train, or on foot. That's just how it is. Because when the audition is over, the pressure is off and you're able to just think like an actor again. But as you get better and better at this, you'll bring that same freedom into the room with you more and more. For now, just know that this is what happens to everyone, and let it go. You weren't going to get the fucking job anyway. Have I said that enough?

OK, this is going to sound cheesy, but I'm going to suggest it anyway. When your audition is over, I'd like to encourage you to celebrate somehow. That's right. It doesn't have to be an all-out bash or anything (that might be a bit indulgent). Maybe it's a double latte instead of a single. Maybe it's going to a movie, buying a treat, or taking a nap. I know an actor who buys himself a bag of Pepperidge Farm Goldfish crackers after every audition. Maybe it's just taking a moment to tell yourself, "Good for you." Listen, I know I said this earlier, but it bears repeating. Not everyone can do this acting stuff. And you just did it—in front of people! And since getting a job is no longer your job, your work is done. Congratulate yourself for accomplishing your task. And then move on to whatever is next. Stop checking your phone.

CHAPTER THIRTEEN

CALLBACKS: THE SIREN SONG

O h, here's a surprise. You have a callback. I have only a few things to say about this stage of the process.

Callbacks are really great compliments. You don't get called back because someone feels sorry for you, or likes you personally, or wants to help your career. You only get called back for one reason: someone thinks you could play this role. And that's pretty damned great. It means you're now in the pool of actors from which they're going to cast it, which is flattering. Callbacks are a great vote of confidence . . . And they should be viewed with tremendous skepticism and mistrust. Because a callback can fool you into thinking the job is nearly yours. And that can stir you up and make you nervous, and you may fall back into the trap of trying to do it right, stand out, "nail it," or—God forbid— book the job. Trust me, it's a nefarious plot. They're trying to trick you, those invisible gremlins that hang about preying on actors' hopes. They're like the Sirens of mythology, beautiful sea nymphs who'd lure sailors to their deaths with their irresistibly enchanting song, drawing ships toward the jagged rocks along the shore. Don't fall for it. Stay in safe waters. Stick to the route. Go do your acting work. That's all you get.

Next, don't change anything from your initial audition. Don't change *anything!* Wear the same outfit, and for heaven's sake, don't change how you're playing the scene. Actors are notorious for finding "new revelations" about a part between the audition and the callback. Trust me. Ignore them. When you're called back, it means that the first person you auditioned for wants other people to see what you did. So show them the same thing you showed the first person. Don't "freshen it up" or "take it up a notch," to keep the first person entertained. Big mistake. Just do what you did.

There's one exception to this. Sometimes, the callback will come with adjustments—"When you come back, make her a little more desperate." "We like the take on the role, but dress more casually." Obviously, these are changes you should make.

Now, really, I hope you'll see this as the easy part. You've already done the work, made the choices, and been given a thumbs up. So don't let the fact that it's a callback gum you up. Don't worry about the fact that there are more people in the room. Larger audience—always good news! Someone saw your show and liked it so much she came back with three friends.

I enjoy going to callbacks. They always make me feel like I just might be a good actor after all. But I know that not everyone enjoys them like I do. If callbacks freak you out, you might need an Audition Psych 101 tune-up before going back in. So just remind yourself of some of the tips we've already discussed and apply them to this part of the process:

- *You're not getting the fucking job.* Don't waste energy getting obsessed over it. Honestly, it's just not going to happen. So what's there to be nervous about?
- Take care of them. Never ask them to take care of you. They're anxious and needy. That gets heightened for them in the callback phase. Let them know it's going to be all right.
- The folks you're meeting aren't scary monsters. They're really hoping to like you. They're rooting for you.
- No one wants to deal with a nervous person. This isn't therapy. You're not allowed to share your nerves.

And remember to bring that life-saving index card with you to the callback so you can remind yourself of the ideas that help you the most.

CHAPTER FOURTEEN

REFLECTIONS ON REJECTIONS

OK, so you've finished your callback, and a few days have gone by, and it turns out they've cast someone else. Tragic? No. It's the norm. They usually cast someone else. Don't beat yourself up. These are just the statistics in this high-supply/low-demand market. Numerical fact: most auditions do not result in jobs.

And since this experience of not getting cast happens with such regularity, I want us to spend some time talking about it.

There are many variables that can affect casting decisions. Here are a few: who had the best performance, who'll work the cheapest, who'll sell tickets, which actors look good together, which friends are owed favors, who fits the subjective tastes of the producers, the actor's personal charm, charisma, familiarity, and/or attractiveness, resemblance to previously cast actors, and so on. Casting is complicated—like creating a patchwork quilt.

So maybe they just didn't like your take on the role. Or maybe it was something else. There are lots of possible reasons why you didn't get cast. Some of them make no sense at all. And yet, even *that*—even casting choices that make no sense—are the norm in our business. Here's a story for you:

Years ago, I was in for a role on the TV show *Cold Case.* It was, on paper, just about the most perfect audition I could ever have. It was for the role of a nebbishy Jewish shoe salesman from Queens, NY. (Sure, it's a stretch.) I loved the role. It was a beautiful scene. And I walk in, and the casting director is sitting there with the director. "Michael Kostroff!" she gushes, "We were just talking about you, and how brilliant you are on *The Wire.*" "We're huge fans," agrees the director. "Is the show back next season?" "Yes, we are," I say. And this goes on for a bit. I feel completely respected and like I belong in the room. And then I read the scene, and because they've now made me feel so welcome and comfortable, I am able to give the performance of a lifetime. You remember when I said actors never think we're good enough and that we're incurably humble? OK, so you can believe me when I tell you, because I don't say it often: that day, I was good! I took my time, I breathed, I had lift-off. Every word . . . every moment . . . hung in the air like a beautiful sparking jewel. I wasn't auditioning. I was the character, having the experience. It was art.

When I was done, there was reverent silence. The casting director and director were moved and misty eyed. They had no comments but "Wow" and "Perfect." They thanked me again and again.

So, when I didn't get the fucking job . . . my manager insisted on finding out what had happened. "What happened?" he asked the casting director. "Michael Kostroff! *The Wire!* You love him! What the hell went wrong?" "Well," she replied, "I am going to hate telling you this story, but you asked . . . so here's the truth: Michael Kostroff left the room, and my director was in awe. 'That's the guy,' he said. But then, a few actors later, in walked a beautiful male model—totally wrong for the part, but our director was completely smitten with the young man. So here's what's happening: the sexy male model will be playing the nebbishy Jewish shoe salesman from Queens."

Now, I'm not telling you this story so you'll feel sorry for me, or outraged at the injustice or lack of artistic integrity. Fuck that. That's the norm, remember? You can't be surprised again and again when show business isn't logical or fair, because that's show business being show business. I'm telling you the story so you can see this: I did my job. Didn't I? I did the very best I could have done. I didn't fail. I succeeded. I just didn't get chosen. What could I do? The director was into the model. It was out of my hands. The element of the process that was *in* my hands was the acting, and in that department—*my* department—I scored an A+.

It's very important that you understand that not getting cast in a role doesn't equal a failure on your part. It doesn't mean you blew it, or that you're not talented, or that you made bad choices. It only means one thing: you didn't get picked. Casting director Sara Isaacson once urged me to communicate this to my classes, saying, "By the time we get to callbacks, we have *several* good choices; they're *all* good. Often we tear our hair out deciding who to pick." Casting director Joy Dewing concurs, "Those final decisions come down to very minor factors, and it's so hard to pick one really terrific actor over another *equally* terrific actor." Are you hearing that? You could not get the job and still have done terrifically well at the audition. Someone chose to go with another actor, that's all.

OK. You're shopping for a shirt. You're going along the rack, looking for possibilities. "Hmmm . . . no . . . no . . . no . . . not my style . . . too bright . . . no . . . no . . . nice!" You check the label—crap—wrong size. Back to looking. "Hmm . . . here we go. Definite possibility." You pull that one out and continue. "Not this one . . . not this one . . . wrong for the occasion . . . aha! Definite possibility." Pull that one out and continue. "Hmm . . . doesn't match the pants . . . hmm . . . not my color . . . no . . . no . . . no . . . great!" At no point in this whole process do you look at the shirts you didn't pick and think, "What *ugly, horrible* shirts. They shouldn't even be on this rack! They're complete failures as shirts, and I'm going to tell everyone not to buy them." Of course not! The other shirts didn't fail, nor were they bad shirts. They just weren't the one you decided on. And that's all casting really is—shopping.

And I really want you to think about the fact that when you don't get the job, someone else does. And it's good news for him or her. If you really want to work on having peace of mind about this stuff, you could choose to celebrate the fact that one of your brothers or sisters in the acting tribe just got a gig. Imagine how excited that person is, getting picked, telling friends, getting to go act somewhere. You could be bitter and jealous, but really, does that have any value at all? Any benefit? None. In fact, those feelings can be detrimental to your future auditions. Going to an audition with the goal of beating someone else out, or showing your competition that you're better than they are (in addition to being kind of a stupid plan) does not result in better auditioning. You're focused on competing rather than acting. Just like trying to get the job, it's completely the wrong goal. But celebrating for the actor who's been cast is very good for your mental health and, I believe, will enhance your whole attitude the next time you go in. Because if you're prepared to celebrate either way, then an audition becomes a win-win proposition, and that makes for a lot less pressure.

I like what the legendary casting director Joy Todd used to say. (Actually I like lots of things she used to say. Joy was a wise, wise woman.) "Sometimes," quoth Joy, "it's someone else's turn."

Generosity of spirit makes it easier for your career to flourish. And so, strange as this may sound, it's rather a practical trait. Cultivate it.

CHAPTER FIFTEEN

Sucky audition? *Disastrously* sucky? Please. You know how many of those I've had? Enough to have convinced me to quit my beloved profession a few dozen times, if I hadn't been such an addict. If you think of it like a quota, you can check one off the list. That's one less sucky audition you're going to have in your career. Hating yourself over it isn't going to make the next one any better. And that's where we want to put our focus now: on the next one, and the next, and the next—a lifetime of better and better audition experiences.

You might not improve by leaps and bounds each time. Take pride in the baby steps.

I have a friend who was, at one time, a psychology student. The professors at her school used to conduct the same experiment with each year's graduating class. And each year, they got the same results. Here's the experiment: ring toss. You know how ring toss works. You throw these rings and try to land them over these stakes in the ground. If a ring lands on the stake that's three feet away, you get five points. If you land it on the stake that's five feet away, you get ten points. Ten feet away, fifteen points. Simple enough, yes? Without exception, the students who wound up with the most points at the end of the game were the ones who just went for the three-foot toss over and over again. The lesson of this experiment is simple. Aiming for what's easy and attainable is a more reliable way to reach success than aiming high and missing. It's become sort of a shorthand expression at my friend's alma mater. When someone is sorting out a big problem or facing a big challenge, a colleague will ask, "What's the three-foot toss?" meaning "What's the small, bite-sized step you know you can achieve? Just do that."

I want you to remember the three-foot toss as you go out into the world and as you go on auditions. Go for improvement, not perfection. If you've been overwhelmed by auditions, don't set a high goal like, "Today, I'm going to do everything I read in Michael's book." Set your goals low. "Today," you might say to yourself, "I'm going to read my index card in the waiting room. That's all." Or, "Today, I'm going to take a walk if there's a long wait." Or "Today, I'm going to make sure I have plans for after my audition." And that's it. Go for improvement, not perfection. Collect the bricks, and build as you go. Baby steps. If you do *slightly* better than last time, that's fantastic.

Just so you know, I have flunked Audition Psych 101 many times, and I teach this stuff. I occasionally find myself, while out in the real world, auditioning, doing things I've been telling actors *not* to do for over a decade: chattering on, apologizing, starting to think I might book the job (the ones I book are rarely the ones I *think* I've booked), evaluating my work while it's happening. And I have to just laugh at myself and try to do better next time.

There are two things I know of that don't cost a dime, but will help you with your audition skills. The first is simply volume. No, I don't mean you should be louder. I mean that you should audition a lot—even if it's hard for you—and amass a volume of audition experiences, because that's one way to cultivate more comfort with the process. Any skill you undertake requires practice, and it's unfair to expect yourself to be completely at ease in an audition situation until you've done it a good number of times. So if you're on the fence about going to an audition, go. You can always use the practice.

The second way I know to get better at auditioning is this. If you ever have an opportunity to sit on the other side of the table and watch auditions, *do not miss that opportunity*. If you can be a reader for a casting director, assist a director, or help friends cast their student films, videos, or theatre projects, you want to do that. Observing auditions teaches you so much, and does so in a way that no class can. You'll see how actors kill their chances at the door, how uncomfortable you feel when someone is nervous, how people tend to apologize as if they have no right to be in the room. It's quite an education.

Once again, I circle back around to my favorite philosophy: you weren't getting the fucking job anyway. Having a sucky audition hasn't killed your chance of booking the role. Math has. The supply-to-demand ratio has. So, while it's fine to feel disappointed if you feel things didn't go well, there are three really, really important things to remember. One is that we are *terrible* at assessing our own work. Listen to me: *T E R R I B L E.* Stop thinking you have any real sense of how you did. Yours is a warped perception. The second thing to remember is that while you're nursing your wounds, beating yourself up, and worrying about your career, the casting folks have completely moved on. I once had an actor ask me, "Should I send an apology?" Good God no. Everyone has moved on. You should too. And the third important thing to remember is . . . say it with me now: you weren't getting the fucking job anyway. Even if you'd been brilliant and perfectly composed, they were always going to pick someone else. A sucky audition just means you didn't enjoy the experience as much as you hope to in the future.

As a saucy friend of mine says whenever she has a breakup with a boyfriend: "Next?"

CHAPTER SIXTEEN

CLOSING THOUGHTS

We've been discussing ways for you to enjoy your auditions more and experience less anxiety. We've been applying some much-needed logic to some of the thoughts that cause unnecessary stress. We've been focused on the *experience* of auditioning. But if you're reading this book, then obviously, you are, or hope to be, a professional actor. And that means that enjoying your auditions isn't enough. You want to work. You want to get cast. Of course you do. There's nothing wrong with that. And of course, we all hope that the result of following my advice is exactly that: more acting work.

But I'm suggesting the following paradox: you don't book acting gigs by wanting them, hoping for them, praying for them, visualizing them, or even (as strange as it sounds) trying to get them.

And there's a simple reason for that—yet another way that our profession is vastly different from others. The teacher applies for a job as a teacher. The contractor applies for a job as a contractor. But ultimately, the job *we're* applying for isn't enthusiastic, talented actor, ready to go to work. It's quirky boss, jilted lover, frustrated mom, drunk patron, competitive salesperson, witness, coach, friend, killer, nurse, scientist, or whoever we are that day.

In order to audition well, you must take your focus completely off the need for employment, approval, and validation, off of the idea of getting it "right," standing out, making an impression, or getting chosen. Instead, you must invest with laser-like intensity in the work of the professional performer: playing your role, adopting your character's needs and goals, finding the truth in your work, offering your art with dignity, and taking care of the people on the other side of the table. All that will free you from the nerves and terror and neediness. It will eliminate that stench of desperation and yes . . . OK, I admit it . . . it *might* enable you to get the job more often than you have in the past. Now, I don't promise that result. But if it turns out to be the case, it might be because it gets the other crap out of the way, freeing you to do the work you're good at and allowing you to present yourself in ways that make it easier for the auditors to see all the reasons why they should cast you.

I follow the exact approach I've shared in this book. And it has served me well.

Even still, since you usually don't get the job (the best mindset in the world can't change the math), you *have* to find a way to be truly satisfied just to be auditioning—just to be sharing your take on a role or a song, giving that gift to the people who are watching, and asking nothing in return. Honestly, it's the only way to keep from going crazy.

In the classic film *Singin' in the Rain*, there's a wonderful fantasy sequence called "Broadway Melody." The great Gene Kelly plays a young hopeful who's just arrived in New York City with nothing but big dreams and a little suitcase. Fresh off the train, he finds his way to a building marked Theatrical Agencies, where he enthusiastically knocks on a hallway door. A grizzled, cigar-smoking agent answers and Gene sings, "Gotta dance!" and then he does, tapping his heart out. The agent slams the door in his face. Undaunted, Gene heads with determination to the next door and does the same for another hard-bitten, big-city agent, who also slams the door in his face. Gene shrugs. No matter. On to the next. All along, there is such great joy in him. He seems so happy just to be dancing. He's just as joyful with the third agent as with the first, because regardless of the outcome, he's doing what he loves. I'm telling you . . . that's kind of the whole key to this stuff.

I like the way Steven Pressfield puts it in his book, *The War of Art*: "The professional . . . reminds himself it's better to be in the arena, getting stomped by the bull, than to be up in the stands or out in the parking lot." We chose this life. No one forced us. Presumably, none of us chose it with the naïve expectation that it would be fair or easy; surely, we knew there'd be auditions, and the disappointment of not getting picked. Even still, I'm so glad I chose this actor's life—not because of the successes I've had, but because it was right for me; it aligns with who I am. I'd rather ride these ups and downs than have an easier time in the wrong profession. And in a certain sense, I never feel more like the itinerant, lifelong, career actor I always dreamed of being than when I suit up, head out, and offer my services at an audition. I hope you'll come to feel the same way.

Here's what I want you to do. Drop me a line and let me know how things go. Nothing would make me happier than knowing that these tips have been helpful to you. OK, my own TV series might make me happier, but only by a little. Hearing of your success ranks reasonably high on my list. So keep me posted. I keep an e-mail account just for that purpose: auditionpsych101@gmail.com.

Remember all that random, unfair, illogical craziness I talked about at the beginning of this book? Well, all that chaos can just as easily work in your favor as against you; you just have to stop trying to control it, get back to doing what you love, and embrace all the lovely lunacy and delicious insanity that is the life of a professional actor.

I have this image I like. I picture myself as a peddler in a little village, like in an old fairytale, wheeling my little wagon of acting through the cobblestone streets, ringing the bell, "Anyone need an actor today? . . . No? . . . Maybe tomorrow, then." . . . and making my way happily along. I say peddle your wares. Wheel your wagon through the streets, ringing your bell. And be happy to be doing that. Be a happy peddler. There's a philosophy in there somewhere.

Here's to your future auditions. Get out there and kill 'em.

EXTRAS

KOSTROFF'S FAVORITE AUDITION TIPS

1. Work on the acting, not the auditioning. What's your character's objective, emotional state, job in the story, et cetera?
2. Always go over your scene out loud with a friend or a coach.
3. Never go to an audition to get cast. Go to enjoy doing what you love. Remember my mantra—"You're not getting the fucking job"—and enjoy the chance to act on a Thursday.
4. Bring your index card with you to every audition.
5. Prepare for your work, then release it. No one suddenly gets more brilliant in the last five minutes before an audition.
6. Use my techniques to fight waiting-room craziness.
7. Keep things in perspective. Remember that there are big, important events happening all over the world. Your audition is tiny by comparison to, say, global warming.
8. This particular audition is not the top of your mountain. You want much more from your career and life. It's a little stepping-stone in the path, not a final goal.
9. Never let your nerves show. No one wants to deal with a nervous actor.
10. Remember the Michael Kostroff Golden Rule of Auditioning: Take care of them. Never ask them to take care of you.
11. Accept that casting directors are regular people trying to do a job. And they're rooting for you.
12. Breathe!

A COLLECTION OF COOL QUOTES

Some of these appear elsewhere in this book, but I wanted you to have them all in one place.

"Actors tend to get in their own way a lot. A lot of times you will do things that will screw up your auditioning process. I loved auditioning, but I was very bad at it for a long period of time. And part of it was because every time I went in on an audition I thought, 'God. I just hope these guys like me' or 'God. I hope I don't screw this up.' And the truth is (having now sat on the other side of that couch) the producers and the director and the writers are all going 'God. I hope this person is the savior. I hope this person does it right.' Every time you go on an audition, you're gambling with house money. From the minute you walk in—you don't have the job—to the minute you walk out—you don't have the job—nothing is different. The only thing that could be different is you get the job. Period. And if you think of it that way, then you will take off all the pressure and you will just go into it going, 'Worst thing that could possibly happen on this audition is I don't get a job that I don't already have.' And once you take that out and do it, I promise you, auditioning is a very different [experience]."
— George Clooney on "Inside the Actors Studio"

"I enjoy auditioning. My advice for getting through it, in all seriousness would be that this may be your only chance in these few minutes to play this part . . . it sometimes helps me to think about it like that. Like, whatever, you know? This is my take on it, this is what I'm doing with it and this is the only time I'll have to get to do it."

—Jim Parsons, as quoted in "Backstage" 11/18/09 (used with permission)

"There's no better place to be in when you walk into an audition than knowing you're not going to get it. Inadvertently, you present your best self."

—Edie Falco, from an interview on Alec Baldwin's "Here's the Thing" podcast

"I look at it as, it's literally your time to be an actor that day. And it's a performance; that's all it is. I don't look at it as a job; it's my time to play the part how I want to play it. And I throw my material away when I leave. You learn to love it."

—Julie Benz, as quoted in "Backstage," 11/18/09 (used with permission)

"It is insane to be in competition with others. Work out a method where you are able to support your friends, your peers, and those with whom you live, while at the same time working very hard to mind your own business and tend to the most important task you have: to improve yourself and use yourself in the best way to earn your place on land. The world will always try to make you think about how you're doing against the others, but ignore this. You need to do—and have to do—the work you were put here to do."

—Arthur Miller, in an interview with James Grissom, 1998

"Treat your career like a bad boyfriend. Here's the thing. Your career won't take care of you. It won't call you back or introduce you to its parents. Your career will openly flirt with other people while you are around. It will forget your birthday and wreck your car. Your career will blow you off if you call it too much. It's never going to leave its wife. Your career is fucking other people and everyone knows but you. Your career will never marry you. Now, before I extend this metaphor, let me make a distinction between career and creativity. Creativity is connected to your passion, that light inside you that drives you. That joy that comes when you do something you love. That small voice that tells you 'I like this. Do this again. You are good at it. Keep going.' That is the juicy stuff that lubricates our lives and helps us feel less alone in the world. Your creativity is not a bad boyfriend. It is a really warm older Hispanic lady who has a beautiful laugh and loves to hug. If you are even a little bit nice to her she will make you feel great and maybe cook you delicious food . . . You have to care about your work but not about the result. You have to care about how good you are and how good you feel, but not about how good people think you are or how good people think you look."

—from *Yes, Please* by Amy Poehler (©2014 by Amy Poehler. Reprinted by permission of HarperCollins Publishers.)

"You have the right to work, but never to the fruit of work."
—The Bhagavad Gita

"There is a vitality, a life force, a quickening that is translated through you into action, and because there is only one of you in all time, this expression is unique. If you block it, it will never exist through any other medium, and be lost. The world will not have it. It is not your business to determine how good it is; nor how valuable it is; nor how it compares with other expressions. It is your business to keep it yours, clearly and directly, to keep the channel open. You do not even have to believe in yourself or your work. You have to keep open and aware directly to the urges that motivate you. Keep the channel open. No artist is ever pleased. There is no satisfaction whatever at any time. There is only a queer, divine dissatisfaction; a blessed unrest that keeps us marching and makes us more alive than the others."
—Martha Graham, as quoted in *Dance to the Piper and Promenade Home* by Agnes de Mille (De Capo Press, 1982)

"I think that the most important thing for an actor is dignity—that an actor has a sense of dignity. And by dignity, I don't mean pride, I don't mean false hope. I don't mean hostility. I mean a sense of the fact that he is in . . . one of the most highly

thought of professions in the history of man. Perhaps one has difficulty getting a credit card—but it's not that kind of dignity that I'm talking about. Each and every person that has ever attended any theatrical or movie adventure . . . has gotten some kind of information that they've been able to apply to their lives . . . And the actor is the source of that. And therefore, when an actor goes on an interview, he doesn't have to be a beggar . . . saying, 'I've got to have this,' no matter how broke he is. He must be willing to be himself at that interview: Not to fake, not to pretend, and not to try to sell a big thing, but to be himself, and to come with a certain dignity, and not to be talked out of that dignity . . . If the actor handles himself with dignity, and with presence . . . he cannot lose, because if it's not this thing, then it will be something else . . . You have got to win—you cannot lose if you come that way."
—Milton Katselas, as quoted in *How to Audition* by Gordon Hunt (used with permission)

"There is such a common level of abuse given to the people who are being interviewed. It's necessary—it's so impor-tant—to turn around to the person who is interviewing you and tell them to go to hell . . . You have to let a creep know when he's being a creep. What happens to actors is that they are treated as talking pieces of meat, who have no other privilege than to act . . . And the fact of the matter is that the overwhelming majority of actors are smarter than the over-whelming majority of the people who are interviewing. So what happens is, after a while, you're being talked to as if you're not there. You're just the body sitting in the chair. You have to say, 'Excuse me. I'd rather not do this job if this

is what I have to go through.' And there's a very specific reason why you do that. It's not just because you want to be a bad guy or a rebel. But very simply: An actor's instrument is himself. And the more you give away . . . the less you have as an actor. Because your soul, your body, is your instrument. So you have to always take the risk . . . You are not giving yourself away, you are not letting yourself be abused, and you are protecting what you have . . . It doesn't make sense to be humble and to be begging and pleading, because that means you are hurting your own work. And eventually, if you do get the part . . . you are not going to have enough resources to play the role."
—Richard Dreyfuss, as quoted in *How to Audition* by Gordon Hunt (used with permission)

"Our deepest fear is that we are powerful beyond measure. It is our light, not our darkness that most frightens us. We ask ourselves, 'Who am I to be brilliant, gorgeous, talented, fabulous?' Actually, who are you *not* to be? You are a child of God. Your playing small does not serve the world. There is nothing enlightened about shrinking so that other people won't feel insecure around you. We are all meant to shine, as children do. We were born to manifest the glory of God that is within us. It's not just in some of us; it's in everyone. And as we let our own light shine, we unconsciously give other people permission to do the same. As we are liberated from our own fear, our presence automatically liberates others."
—Marianne Williamson

"Nerves and butterflies are fine—they're a physical sign that you're mentally ready and eager. You have to get the butterflies to fly in formation, that's the trick."
—Steve Bull

"The most important trait I encourage in actors is to know their self worth. I am pretty sure this is not taught in acting school, and it is a trait that is essential to a successful career in the commercial acting world . . . Remember, a lack of self worth equals desperation, the ultimate repellent of bookings and people. Agents, producers and casting directors want to work with people who are their equals; someone who knows they have something to bring to the table. When meeting with potential agents, you are looking to form a partnership, not get something from them. Someone who has a strong sense of self worth knows they have something to offer and appears as someone who will be easy to work with. Lack of self worth can come across as someone who will be needy and difficult to work with."
—Robin Harrington, commercial agent (www.agentwithachirp.com)

"We work in the dark. We do what we can. We give what we have. Our doubt is our passion and our passion is our task. The rest is the madness of art."
—Henry James

SPEECHES FOR THE NUMBERS EXERCISE

"This is the happiest day of my life. I will never forget this moment, standing here, taking it all in. I can hardly believe I'm finally going to be a published writer. It's all I've ever wanted. And now, after such a long climb, I'm at the top of the mountain, looking at a bright new future. My lifelong dream has finally come true."

"I remember how it started. We were just sitting around, complaining, and we came up with this plan to scare Alan. He'd been a real jerk. No one liked him. And one thing led to another and . . . well . . . you know what happened. We killed Alan. And I'm glad we did. He was mean to everyone, and we're all glad he's gone."

"I want to propose a toast to the greatest lady I've ever known. Katherine is wise, hilarious, and the most supportive and reliable friend anyone could ever ask for. Now, I know she gets embarrassed, so I won't go on. I'll just say this: Katherine, I hope you know how deeply you are loved and appreciated around here. You're our friend, and we thank you for everything you've done, and everything you are."

"I hate you. I've always hated you. Everything about you bothers me—your stupid face, and that stupid way you talk. You drive me crazy. Why can't you just shut the hell up and go away?"

"Listen, I was just wondering . . . I mean, I know I don't know you. But, I mean, you look nice. I mean, you look like a nice person. Would you—and you can say no if you like—would you be into, like, having coffee or something? If not, that's cool. I just thought I'd ask."

"I'm sick to death of poverty. I'm sick of people begging in the streets, kids not getting proper educations, crime going unchecked. I'm sick of our young people feeling lost and directionless. I'm sick of our citizens feeling like no one is listening and no one cares. I care. Our citizens deserve better lives. And that's why I'm running for governor."

"This is the living room, of course. It's a bit smaller than some of the other properties we looked at, but the view is really something. And it gets excellent light. As you see, there are many of the original features: molding, built-in shelves, some of the fixtures. They even have the old glass doorknobs, which is nice. Now let's move into the den, and let me know if you have any questions."

"As I'm sure you can understand, I'm shocked. All this time I think we're building something together—our dream project, the one we talked about for years—and now I find out my own partner is stealing from me. My friend. I mean, how do you sleep at night? How do you live with yourself? Is this the person you want to be? I have nothing else to say. Take your money. Live it up."

"Henrietta Morgan was nowhere near Webster's Creek on the day in question. We have the written testimony of her physician that she's incapable of climbing more than a few steps at a time, and that she faints at the sight of blood. And then, there's her own cooperation with the authorities. Yes, she hated Rebecca Franklin. Hated her with a passion. But she didn't kill her. And I intend to prove that."

"You have got to meet my crazy friend, Rhonda. She's like . . . party central. Whenever Rhonda calls with a plan, we say yes. Because it always ends up being *so* much more fun than you ever knew you could have. She's a maniac. Once, we even got ourselves arrested . . . and it was *still* one of the best nights of my life. So, tonight, I'm picking you up at 9:30— no argument. And we'll see what she has in store for us. It's going to be crazy."

I am not going to let you give up. You hear me? You've worked way too hard for this. And if you let this one, insignificant little setback throw you off course, you might miss out on the greatest adventure of your life. Everything you've worked for could be waiting just around the next turn. But if you give up now, you'll never know. So you are going to cross the finish line, even if I have to drag you there myself."

"The man I work for doesn't like it when people are disloyal. He sent me here to tell you that. The last person who broke a promise disappeared mysteriously. Funny how that happens. Now, I'm not saying that's gonna happen to you. I'm just saying . . . if it does, you won't even see it coming. You'll just be here one day and then . . . poof . . . you'll be gone. You get me?"

RECOMMENDED READING AND VIEWING

<u>Books</u>

How to Audition by Gordon Hunt

How to Get the Part without Falling Apart by Margie Haber

The Actor Takes a Meeting by Stephen Book

actor. writer. whatever. by Mellini Kantayya (a funny, insightful perspective on the artist's life)

Bright-sided: How Positive Thinking is Undermining America by Barbara Ehrenreich

Backwards and Forwards by David Ball (a brilliant little book on analyzing your text)

Audition by Michael Shurtleff

<u>Documentaries</u>

Every Little Step (2008) - Follows the audition process for the 2006 Broadway revival of *A Chorus Line.*

Casting About (2005) - A lyrical documentary about the experience of casting actresses for a dramatic film.

ABOUT THE
AUDITION PSYCH 101 WORKSHOP

Since 2006, I've been offering the Audition Psych 101 workshop every chance I get. The live format allows for several things that the book doesn't. In particular, there's a dynamic that happens when actors gather in a group and realize that they're not alone in their anxieties and weird ideas about auditioning. That in itself is liberating.

If you'd like to be notified of workshops in your area, visit the Audition Psych 101 website (www.auditionpsych101.com) and subscribe. I maintain discrete mailing lists for each city or region and do my best to schedule workshops wherever my acting career takes me.

If you're interested in organizing an Audition Psych 101 workshop in your area, there are several ways to do that. In the past, I've been hosted by theatre companies, acting schools, universities, and actor cooperatives. I've also arranged local workshops independently. Contact me at auditionpsych101@gmail.com and we'll see what we can figure out.

ABOUT THE AUTHOR

Michael Kostroff has waited tables, answered switchboards, been a bank teller, a proofreader, a customer service rep, and a theme park entertainer.

These days he's a working television and stage actor, best known for his five seasons as the unscrupulous gang attorney Maury Levy on HBO's acclaimed hit *The Wire*. His extensive list of other TV and film credits can be found at www.imdb.com. Kostroff's stage work has included leading roles at some of the nation's top regional theatres. As an original cast member of the first national tour of *The Producers*, he understudied the starring role of Max Bialystock, a part he has since played in productions all over the country. He also toured as the comically evil Thénardier in *Les Misérables*, recreating the role for the 25th anniversary production.

As a writer, Kostroff's work has been wide-ranging. He's written magazine articles, song lyrics, live shows, stand-up comedy, theatre reviews, special events, and more. From 2006-2012 he served as advice columnist for the actors' newspaper *Backstage*, fielding questions from performers nationwide on an endless variety of topics for the weekly "Working Actor" column. Kostroff's first book, *Letters from Backstage* (Allworth Press, 2005), is a funny, honest, behind-the-scenes chronicle of his life on the road with *The Producers* and *Les Misérables*.

In 2006, Kostroff began teaching his Audition Psych 101 workshop. In the years since, he's had the opportunity to present the class to actors all over the country. He's also taught workshops on comedic acting, improvisation, on-camera technique, and the business of "the business."

He currently resides in his hometown of New York City, where he wastes considerable amounts of time playing online Scrabble. He has one wife, two stepchildren, and a cat.

Made in United States
North Haven, CT
29 December 2021